JILL FARMER

THERE'S
NOT
ENOUGH
TIME

. . . and other lies we tell ourselves.

Acknowledgements

In a life where you feel like there is never enough time, taking the time to read a book on a subject that feels uncomfortable and unsolvable is a testament to the light that shines in you that wants to illuminate a clearer path. So, first and foremost, I want to acknowledge that light in you and say I truly believe great things are coming for you, if you are willing to leave behind the stuff that isn't serving you.

To my fabulous pre-readers, Bridgette, Beth, Eric, Shannon, Anne, Kimberly, Nancy, Michelle and more, your insight and support helped me get over the hump. Words can't express my gratitude.

To Angela, the coach who believed in this book way, way before I did, thanks for your brilliance, ideas, honesty and support.

To my MBI coaching tribe, your amazing intelligence, generosity and intuitive gifts never cease to amaze me. Thank you for enveloping me in your love and energy at every turn.

To my outstanding clients, who teach me more every single session than I could learn anywhere else.

To my unbelievable parents, thank you for always believing in me and encouraging me to go for it. Your faith in me has always been one of the greatest gifts in my life.

To my outrageously supportive and fun in-laws, siblings and the rest of my extended family, thanks for being excited and encouraging cheerleaders on this and all of my other journeys.

To my fabulous friends from childhood, high school, college, work, the childrearing years, and now; I am incredibly blessed to have each and every one of you in my life. I am so grateful for the joy, support, adventures and fun you have shared.

Finally, the biggest thanks goes to my husband and kids. Thank you for letting me surrender to the computer to make this dream be born.

About confidentiality: As a coach, it's paramount for me to protect and honor the confidentiality of my clients. The anecdotes you see in this book are either melded characters that exemplify common traits or experiences I observed in several people, or they are from clients or friends who have given me express permission to share their stories. I want to express deep thanks to all who have shared their experiences and expertise in this book.

To John
For teaching me
there's always
more than enough

There's Not Enough Time
... and other lies we tell ourselves

Jill Farmer
Lake Time Press

Published by Lake Time Press
Copyright ©2012 Jill Farmer

Editor: Lynn Hess

Cover and Interior Design:
www.DavisCreative.com

Library of Congress Cataloging-in-Publication Data
Library of Congress Control Number: 2012918365

Jill Farmer
There's Not Enough Time
... and other lies we tell ourselves

ISBN: 978-0-9882881-0-2
Library of Congress subject headings:
1. Business   2. Motivational   3. Time Management   4. Self Help

Table of Contents

Foreword

In this book, Jill tackles what is perhaps the biggest lie of a Western woman's life: I don't have enough time. But, here's the thing about Jill—she's a realist. She understands you have a mile-long to-do list. And, in the heyday of too much too-doing, she had one that was *two* miles long. But I digress; as I was saying, Jill's a realist. It's not enough that she lets us in on the little-known secret that "I don't have enough time" is a big fat lie, she also gives us all concrete tools for doing it differently. Concrete. Meaning tools that are practical, do-able, and in the end a heck of a lot more effective than the spinning we do (and when I say we I of course mean I) when we're overwhelmed.

Now if you *like* frantically bouncing from one thing to another, or bolting awake in the middle of the night with another bout of anxiety, or forgetting your first-grader at the school pick-up line (all the while thinking, "Why can't this kid drive yet for Pete's sake!?!"), then this book is not for you.

If however, you are tired, so deeply tired, of being on the treadmill of checking off meaningless tasks on your list in search of that elusive sense of peace, then I suggest you put reading this book at the top of your to-do list immediately. Jill's tools are not just the same old collection of "suck it up and try harder!" Because really, if that worked, wouldn't you have it nailed by now? What I love about this book is that Jill gets to the source of the "there's not enough time" story (Spoiler alert! It's a story.) and gives you tools that will help you change your relationship with time.

Are you scratching your head at the idea that you have a *relationship* with time? Exactly. What Jill does here is help you bring a deep awareness of how you're spending time—where you stop yourself dead in your tracks with overwhelm, or where you're a whirling dervish of perpetual motion hoping that by frantically accomplishing, there will be finally time for you—and shows you how to shift your dysfunctional relationship with time into something more satisfying, peaceful, and yes, productive.

A word of warning: Some of these exercises will make your to-do-list-loving self break out in sweaty hives or may really chap your hide. My tip for you is to see if you can suspend that part of you that is afraid of or cynical about change long enough to try the exercises out. Because if you do, they can transform your life.

Bridgette Boudreau
CEO of Martha Beck International
Master Life Coach

Introduction

Life Is the Journey, Not the Milestones…

or the stuff you cross off your list.

You might classify my prim neighbor slipping on cat vomit in my dining room, our laptop's violent explosion caused by a buildup of unread e-mails, and dropping our daughter off at camp two weeks before counselors arrived as a series of unrelated (albeit unfortunate) events.

But they were all related—related to my lack of time. Who has the luxury of enough time to clean up the cat puke, read all the e-mails, and remember mundane details like camp start dates?

Not me!

Life was just too busy.

There was not enough time.

I'll bet you have the overstuffed schedule, frenzied pace, and constant overwhelm to prove it, too. I get it. I've been there. Not so long ago, I would wake up in my comfy bed every morning thinking, "It's good to be alive. It's great to be me."

That sense of delicious contentment would last for about 1.2 seconds.

Then, I would remember. It would hit me like a punch in the gut.

I had too much to do.

I. Didn't. Have. Enough. Time.

My family heard it from me at every turn:

"You've got to hurry."

"Can't you see there's too much for me to do?"

"I don't have time for this, honey!"

"We're late!"

"Sweetheart, I'd love to hear about that, but there's just no time right now."

I didn't *want* to constantly bark clipped orders at my beloveds. I longed for peace, leisure, and ease. But my plate was just too full to relax.

An annoyingly calm and collected friend once called me a whirling dervish of frenetic movement. Even more maddening? Though I was constantly in motion, I seldom enjoyed a sense of closure or accomplishment at the end of the day.

My overplayed anthem had a bunch of tired old refrains:

It's such a busy time right now.

I have so much to do.

There is not enough time.

Or… is there?

When you think the thought **there's not enough time,** your body may respond with a clenched jaw, throbbing shoulders, an aching neck, or even a slightly nauseated feeling in your stomach. You may start early in the morning, and remain in motion until you hit the pillow at night. Or, you may be paralyzed, overwhelmed by your interminable to-do list, and unsure where to start.

This book is for anyone who feels like there's not enough time to do everything that needs to get done. It will help you see your situation with a fresh perspective, a new set of lenses. You'll learn new tools and sharpen skills to help you shape a clearer picture of your priorities.

Then, you will be more likely to accomplish the things that have meaning and impact in your life, as opposed to just frantically bouncing from one thing to the next with nothing to show for it.

Most important, you will learn ways to be kinder to your-self, and to create time to take care of yourself. You'll discover ideas for dissolving dreaded tasks that stop you cold, put you in a bad mood, or cause you to procrastinate and derail other areas of your life that have meaning and purpose for you.

You will also learn how your mind is subconsciously sabotaging big chunks of your time. I'll show you how these tools have helped all kinds of people, from surgeons to stay-at-home moms, regain more time to do what they want. This book is *not* an efficiency primer designed to dictate a system that will make you "better."

Chances are, you've tried that already and it just made you feel worse. This is about a new way of thinking to help you feel saner and more connected to the things that matter to you most.

Jill

Chapter 1

The Circumstance Story

For decades, I dreamed of a fantasy windfall of *more time*. This jackpot of time always loomed in the future.

In high school, I "just needed to get to college," where I would create my own leisurely class schedule and lounge around looking collegiate.

That didn't pan out so well. College was a little more hectic than I imagined. Balancing a full load of classes, trying to get good grades, joining every committee to form every committee to create the committee, and working part-time ate up enormous amounts of my time. I had the weight gain, "alcohol to unwind" habit, and excessive caffeine consumption to prove it.

Next, I believed getting a real job was going to fix my time crunch. I would have nothing to do in the evenings and on weekends except relax with my husband, who would take over *half* of my responsibilities, which would give me *twice* as much time. Ah, the bliss!

Only once I plunged into the whitewater rapids of my first newsroom, I discovered life as a fledgling TV reporter (with a lot to prove) wasn't structured with much down time. Being a new wife didn't afford me oodles of leisure, either. Instead, it created a fun new tug-of-war over the best ways to use *our* time.

So, I fantasized about being an anchor. Anchors had time to microwave popcorn at their desks and reapply their foundation, for God's sake. That was the gig I needed in order to capture more time.

Alas, the anchor chair just meant more responsibilities, more at stake, and the need for perfect hair and makeup (never my strong point *and* surprisingly time-consuming.)

Kids, though a joyous addition to my life, proved to be the most enormous time suckers of all. So, I decided to work part-time, which would give me the luxury of a meaningful career and the "lackadaisical life of a mommy" a few days a week.

Turns out I was wrong about my days "off." On my frenzied days at home, I wore yoga pants because there didn't always seem to be time to zip the zipper on my jeans. I blamed my insanity on the never-ending juggle of work and home responsibilities.

So, after lots of contemplation, and a few sleepless nights, I decided to give up my career in TV, and stay home full-time with the girls. *Finally,* I would have the time to be the parent I wanted to be, grow organic food, exercise for hours a day, and be the best wife, daughter, Lutheran, friend, yogi, and just plain human being who ever lived.

That bubble burst the week after I quit my job.

None of my fantastic plans for at-home-greatness came to fruition. At the end of six months, I was more dazed and frazzled than I'd ever been. My house was a mess, I gained weight, I felt sluggish, and I was a tense, crabby wife and mother. On top of it all, I couldn't seem to get anything meaningful done. When the drastic measure of leaving my career had failed to solve my time crisis, I had to face reality.

It wasn't my circumstances that had me fried.

It was my story: the story that something *external* was going to happen to me to fix my never-ending time shortage.

I had been telling myself for *so long* that there was some magic treasure trove of time waiting for me in a future situation in my life; it hit me like a ton of bricks to realize that might not be true.

What's your story?

My Story...

When things first started getting hectic in my life, I was

_____ .

That's when I told myself things would get less hectic/
I'd have more time when _____

_____ .

Did you get more time?_____yes _____no (If yes, congrats! If no, keep going.)

When that happened, and I was busier than ever, I
thought it would get easier after _____ .

Did you get more time?_____yes _____no
(If yes, congrats! If no, keep going.)

When that didn't work out, it was that I just needed

_____

to happen and things would calm down.

Did you get more time?_____yes _____no
(If yes, congrats! If no, keep going.)

Today, I just want _____ to happen so I can be

_____ .

What does your story reveal to you? _____

_____

_____ .

How is this story holding you back? _____

_____

_____ .

Interesting. Let's get going on ways you can start getting more time in your life right now.

Meet Sandy.

See if anything in her story sounds familiar.

Sandy

Age: 38

Occupation: Physician

Single Mother of 9-year-old twins

When did you first notice things getting hectic/ overwhelming?

I remember life getting really hectic for me in undergrad.

I told myself I'd have more time when...

I graduated from medical school.

That didn't happen?

No. So, I thought it would calm down after residency. I thought once I established a practice I could drastically cut down on my hours.

And, after residency?

I was busier than ever.

What does your story reveal to you?

That way of thinking made me put off being good to myself. I told myself I needed to wait until I'd achieved the next thing in order to exercise, pursue my hobbies, or enjoy other things I liked doing. It's a curse of many goal-oriented people.

How did this story hold you back?

By the time I had my twins, I had finally figured out that no circumstance was going to suddenly emerge where I finally had more time to do the things I wanted. I knew I needed to reframe my perspective. The situation didn't need to change; I needed to change my thinking.

Now?

*I've learned that, regardless of what's going on, **now** is the time to make my life what I want it to be, instead of waiting for a time 10 years from now.*

Today, I understand it's important, right now, to take care of myself and include things in my life that I thoroughly enjoy. I try to teach my medical students that life is not something to be to be experienced and enjoyed "when they're done." It's for now. It's about making the best of today.

No Time to Parent?

Kids have a way of exacerbating our time issues. When we're in the thick of parenting young children, we convince ourselves that the next stage in their lives will give us more freedom and ultimately more time will rain from the sky. It's true that ages birth through five years require an enormous amount of constant supervision and that as our kids get more independent we don't have to be in the same shared space with them as much.

However, in my experience, each childhood stage represents a different kind of time obligation for parents. There's no bathing or dressing or bum wiping required from me anymore. But I practically need a residency permit in my car because I spend so much darn time carting kids these days. Friends with kids off at college or out on their own report continuing to spend far more time on family-related stuff than they thought they would be at this stage in life.

As parents, when we feel overwhelmed and underachieving, we wish we could choose to work less, or parent less, or housekeep less. But those don't feel like options.

It is a quandary.

"I need my job to cover expenses."

"Spend less hands-on time with my kids? They'll be drugs addicts or prostitutes by the age of sixteen."

"Reduce my obligations? Everyone will think I'm unwilling to pull my weight."

If we're not careful, we can miss out on some pretty amazing parenting moments as we wish away our time. And, even if we're not parents, we can miss out on a whole lot of life if we are constantly looking at the next situation or circumstance in our lives to bring us more time.

We tie ourselves in knots. So, let's begin to loosen up the snarl. We'll start with your to-do list.

Chapter 2

The To-Do List Makeover
Part One

The Overloader

My friend Lynn, a cardiologist and one of the smartest people I know, had a dirty little secret. She used her to-do list to should all over herself. Shoulding all over ourselves (to borrow a popular term from AA meetings) is when that critical voice in our head tells us what we should have done, or should be doing now, or what we should do in the future, to be better.

"I never get everything done on my list," Lynn lamented over coffee one morning.

Curious, I asked to see it. Lynn proceeded to unfold a piece of well-worn paper that may have originally come over on the Mayflower. She had scrawled on every inch of white space with minuscule print, spelling out countless tasks and reminders of things she needed to do and things she *should* be doing. My mouth gaped open at the sheer volume of text.

This wasn't a list. It was a diatribe.

I talk to lots of folks who vomit up every single item they would *ever* need to complete in order to be decent parents, professionals, spouses, volunteers, citizens, and human beings onto documents they call their to-do lists.

Then, every time they pull out these dissertations they have proof in black and white that they are not good enough. It doesn't matter that they would need to transcend the time/space continuum in order to complete half of the tasks they have assigned themselves in any given week. *The list* is an ever-present reminder of their inadequacy.

When I make a ridiculously onerous to-do list (and believe me, I do), it lets my primal fears be true. "I can't possibly ever get this all done" is a fabulous partner to the host of other "not good enough" thoughts that my inner critic loves to circulate in my mind like a vicious spin cycle.

Putting all of these shoulds on paper gives us the illusion we're organizing. In reality, it's just using a pen to give voice to that nasty mean voice in our head. The to-do list is a good thing, until it starts making you feel bad.

Those of us who are chronic to-do list overloaders feel a strong current of gnawing angst. We are driven to cross things off the list, and feel too guilty to rest or take a break. We often feel resentful, overwhelmed, exhausted, and burned out. We live under the delusion that someday we'll get it *all* done. However, at the end of every single day, we beat ourselves up for all the things we should have completed.

Author Brooke Castillo says, "The reason people quit is because they look at how far they have to go instead of how far they've come."

That, my friends, is shoulding all over yourself via your to-do list. It doesn't help you get more done. It makes things worse. An overloaded to-do list is unbelievably inefficient— and worse, it's not a nice way to treat yourself. Can you imagine managing employees with never-ending lists that did nothing but confuse and discourage? They would quit in a minute.

Overloaders, unite. I am living proof you can completely revamp your to-do list. You can make it drastically shorter, clearer, and kinder without having your life implode around you. On the contrary, you may be shocked at how much freer, more accomplished, and at peace you can become when you use your to-do list for something other than self-abuse.

The Freestyler

A few of you have been skimming along, secretly thinking "It sucks to be them. I've got my to-do list right here," punctuated with a couple of taps to your skull.

That means you're a to-do list freestyler. A freestyler is someone who does not write lists down. Instead, you keep three, four, or five lists going on simultaneously in your head. While quick to point out the futility of a to-do list, freestylers are often the most frazzled of us all. Keeping a list in your head would be a grand idea, if our minds weren't, as bestselling author Martha Beck says, as unreliable as "a two-bit whore."

Time management guru David Allen, in his bestselling book "Getting Things Done," says, "Your conscious mind, like a computer screen, is a focusing tool, not a storage place. You can only think about two or three things at once." As soon as something new grabs our attention, the list of things we wanted to remember gets blasted to smithereens.

Ever gone to the supermarket with a few things in mind? Then, when you get to the car, you realize you only picked up one of those original items, even though you just bought 12 bags of perishables? That list in your head got erased as soon as you saw your favorite potato chips on sale for $1.69.

Freestylers have great intentions. But, by not writing things down, you are sabotaging your efforts to get things done. You end up using tons of mental energy beating your-self up for forgetting things, or "being all over the place."

I have the distinct gift of being an overloader *and* a freestyler.

Confessions of My Freestyling

My daughters had just flown off to Florida for three sunny spoiled days with their grandparents. Right after their plane took off, I mentally constructed my to-do list. It included:

1. *Spring Cleaning of the entire house: Complete with laundering every stitch of bedding, vacuuming the mattresses, organizing all closets, removal and wipe down of every item in the kitchen, and more.*

2. *Work stuff: Write life-changing blogs, find new clients, write mind-blowing speech, read one hour (solid!) of dense, intense research material, conceptualize and create video blog.*

3. *Work out for an hour every day (minimum!!!!) and have romantic, relationship-deepening evenings with my husband, to be enjoyed after completion of above list.*

About 45 minutes into my "relaxing" three days, I was discombobulated, to say the least. I hadn't even put a single coffee mug in the dishwasher, let alone started tackling the cacophony of tasks banging around in my head.

I did not have a written list, a roadmap to help me create a reasonable agenda for my available time. So, I was scattered, distracted, frustrated, and immobile.

Productivity expert Paul H. Burton calls making lists "core dumps"—a way to get rid of the tasks swirling in your head to get quieter and more focused. He says, "Once your mind knows that these items have been captured, it can let go of them and turn its full attention to what needs doing right now."

"My to-do list helps me stay in my lane," explains branding expert Laurie Foley. She says when she uses her list it helps her remain focused and stick to her intentions.

My real concern with freestyling it? You never get to be done. There are always shoulds floating around in your mind. Prioritizing allows you to decide on the most important stuff to get done. Your to-do list provides a framework for those priorities. When that's finished, it's time to *be done*. (More on that later.)

Whether you're a recovering overloader, a freestyler, or a little of both, let's remake your to-do list to be a friend, not a foe.

To-Do List Makeover Tool #1—
Get rid of 2-minute tasks.

One of the things I hear constantly from clients? Annoying little tasks keep them from getting more important stuff done. These pesky jobs distract and destroy any chance they have at sticking to one thing long enough to complete it.

Or...

They become engrossed in bigger tasks, which keeps them from getting around to the minor stuff that then piles up. This conundrum is a major contributor to an overloaded to-do list *and* a cause of freestyler mayhem. Here's a simple way to solve that problem.

If anything on your to-do list can be done in less than a couple of minutes, it belongs on your 2-minute task list. Before you create your to-do list for the day, write down no more than five 2-minute tasks.

Example 2-Minute Task List:

1. Call and schedule my hair appointment
2. Pick up toys in TV room and put in bin
3. Reply to Evite
4. Write check for yard guy
5. Put old sweater in giveaway pile.

Your 2-Minute Task List:

1. _____

2. _____

3. _____

4. _____

5. _____

Then, set a timer. This is *really* important. Set your timer for 10 minutes. No more than 10 minutes. Not kidding. Seriously, 10 minutes. Then, spend those 10 minutes (or less) doing *only* the items on your 2-minute list. No launching into other things. No "I'll just do this little extra task while I'm here." Stick to your 2-minute task list.

This is a fabulous way to clear the air of those irksome little things that buzz around in your head to distract and dissuade you from getting more meaningful stuff accomplished. The timer is key.

Make it into a game. Blast your favorite music while you tackle your 2-minute tasks. Make it energizing, even fun. Getting little things out of the way makes it much easier to get clearer on the other stuff you want to get done.

To-Do List Makeover Tool #2—
The Rule of Five

After you've gotten rid of those blasted 2-minute tasks, the most important change you can make is to reduce and simplify your regular to-do list. The easiest way to do that is the Rule of Five.

The Rule of Five is keeping your daily to-do list to five items.

Yup, I said five.

I know, I know. For some of you, cutting your list to five things sounds drastic, even downright irresponsible. When I first started experimenting with this, I was fairly certain that I would immediately be inducted into the bad mom/wife/person Hall of Fame if I dared to place only a paltry five items on my list. As is often the case, I was dead wrong.

Now I know cutting my to-do list to five items is one of the most powerful steps I can take to be more productive *and* content. It feels good. And, it works. That's why I want you to try it.

The purpose of your to-do list is not to warehouse all of the angst-producing tasks and duties in your life. It is to help you track and remember action items that you'd like to get done, today. To-do lists are for today. You can even call it your to-day list, if that floats your boat.

Overloaders may need to cut down their list in stages. I'll walk you through it.

Jill's To-Do List

Take a look at your current to-do list and pick out the MOST pressing or pertinent items on it. Only include items that have a deadline, or are most important to your peace of mind. Here's mine:

- Return library books
- Go to grocery store
- Book plane tickets
- Exercise
- Laundry
- Plan kitchen remodel
- Fill gas tank
- Figure out summer camp schedule

To-Do List

Take a look at your current To-Do list and pick out the MOST pressing or pertinent items on it. Only include items that have a deadline, or are most important to your peace of mind. (Don't worry—coming up, I'll tell you what to do with all of the items you are leaving off this list.)

_____

_____

_____

_____

_____

_____

_____

_____

_____

Once you have your rough draft, our next step is to make sure you actually accomplish what's on your list. For that you'll need a calendar. You can use a good old-fashioned paper calendar, your beloved planner (as long as it lists the hours in the day), or your favorite electronic calendar. I strongly recommend viewing electronic versions (like Outlook or iCal) on a desktop computer screen, as opposed to just on your smartphone. This gives you a clear, honest picture of your available time.

Take a look at the *actual* time you have available for the day, and calmly and curiously notice what items on your to-do list can be achieved, given your available time (more on how to achieve that calm and curious state coming up in Chapters 4 & 5).

Here's How

Here's the process I used to make my to-do list for today. Booking plane tickets is top priority. Based on work and family commitments throughout the day, exercise will work best in the morning.

Since there is a *specific* time of day when this needs to be accomplished, I am not going to put exercise on my to-do list. It goes on my calendar. This way, I have a specific action item at a specific time. Just putting exercise somewhere on the list makes it unlikely to get squeezed in my day.

Library books and getting gas also make the list. I'm not going to put them in a specific time on the calendar, because I have some different options for when I could do these. They stay on my to-do list as reminders when time becomes available.

Looking at my available time, I realize I can't finish all

of the laundry currently piled up in my laundry room. But I could get two loads washed and dried. Finally, the grocery store is feeling pretty pertinent. (I'm pretty industrious, but I don't think I can make a meal out of barbecue sauce, butter, and celery, the only items currently in my fridge.)

Now, sticking to my **Rule of Five**, here's my new To-Do List:
- Book Plane tickets
- Fill gas tank
- Return library books
- 2 loads of laundry
- Go to Grocery Store

Now, it's your turn. Using your calendar to look at the _actual time available_, create your to-do list for today. Remember The Rule of Five (and don't panic, I'll tell you what to do with the items that don't belong on this list in a minute.)

To-Do List for _____ **(date)**

_____

_____

_____

_____

_____

Using your calendar to accurately measure your actual time available is the most important key. As my friend Megan put it, "I can do five things that won't take that long, one thing that will take all of my time, or a combination of two or three things. But I need to stay realistic in my expectations." That conscious awareness has increased Megan's contentment and her productivity.

To-Do List Makeover Tool #3— What to do with the items you took off your list

The Rule of Five helps convert an inefficient list full of things you never seems to get done, and distills it into action items you're highly likely to complete. Now, what should you do with all of the items that don't make it on to your to-do list for today?

Calendar

Anything with a specific future date goes on your calendar. You'd be surprised how many people put *2pm Wednesday Dr. appointment* on their to-do list, and then are shocked when they forget it.

But what about items that are *not* date-specific? If you'd like to get something done and you don't have time today, put it on your calendar for tomorrow or another day when you will have time to complete it. That is *not* procrastination. It is efficiency. You're far more likely to get it done that way.

Mark Twain once said, "Never put off till tomorrow what you can do the day after tomorrow." A plastic surgeon friend tells me one of the geniuses in her field uses a similar quote to train his protégés. His theory? It's better to create realistic scenarios about what you *really* need to get done in the *here and now*, so you can bring a clear mind to the operating table. If it's good enough for leading surgeons, it's good enough for me.

Tasks that repeat (daily or otherwise) belong on your calendar, assigned to a specific time of day. As I mentioned, my success rate for exercising goes way up when I put it on my calendar instead of hiding it on my overloaded to-do list or letting it bang around in my head.

But don't fall into the trap of scheduling every single minute of your day. You simply have to leave space in your calendar for unexpected things to pop up. Remember, the gaps in your calendar are the times for you to complete what's on your to-do list. If it's completely jam-packed, you're setting yourself up to fail.

Big Projects

Once you have moved time- or date-specific tasks from your list and put them on your calendar, you will probably have some items left. Scan through the list looking for big projects. They are jobs that require multiple steps and take more time than you have available today to complete.

- Remodeling the kitchen
- Teaching your neighbor to read
- Figuring out the entire summer camp schedule for your kids
- Losing 30 pounds
- Solving global warming

These would all be examples of big projects. They are also things I may have once had on my to-do list (clearly, before it had undergone its makeover.) In Chapter 7, you'll learn how to tackle big projects that have been hanging over your head for years. It's exhilarating and freeing. So, hang around for it.

For now, simply:

1. Write down the title of your big project on a single piece of paper.
2. Slip that paper into a file folder (or hanging folder) titled "Big Projects."

A giant goal on your list looms as a fear-mongering reminder of all you "still have to do." Big projects don't belong on your daily to-do list.

To-Do List Makeover Tool #4— Prioritizing

Even when you take out the 2-minute tasks, events with specific time frames, and the big projects, deciding what to do (and in what order) can be a challenge. The late Steven Covey, in his bible for self-improvement "The 7 Habits of Highly Effective People," had a fabulous quadrant concept for prioritizing tasks. Inspired by his work, I have developed what I call the prioritization zones.

Prioritization Zones

The Stress-Out Zone

- Urgent matters
- Unexpected crises
- Medical emergencies
- Pressing problems
- Deadline-driven stuff
- Last-minute preparations for scheduled activities

Lots of the items in this zone are necessary. However, they can take over your life if you're not aware and conscious. Spend too much time in this zone, and you will be BURNED OUT.

Manage by being mindful.
Delegate. Barter. Plan. Organize.

The Hamster-on-the-Wheel Zone
- Interruptions
- Some phone calls
- Constant e-mail checking
- Some meetings
- Many "pressing" matters

This is where we get deceived. We get sucked into "doing"—and this zone can trap us if we're not careful. We're constantly moving, and not going anywhere. This is why 2-minute tasks are so important. We keep the little stuff in a container, so it doesn't leak out into other areas and take over.

Avoid when possible. Be specific about and limit the amount of time you spend doing any of the tasks listed above.

The Procrastination Zone
- Busywork
- Junk e-mail
- Frittering away hours on social media (Facebook, Twitter, and Pinterest)

- Escape activities that don't bring any joy or purpose
- Mindless TV and internet surfing that doesn't make you feel good
- Arguments and petty conflicts
- Gossip

This zone is where we hide out. We take cover here to avoid making progress or if we fear not being perfect. More on how to avoid staying here in Chapter 6.

Avoid completely. Period.

The Productive Zone

- Preparation/Planning
- Prevention
- Values clarification
- Creativity
- Exercise, healthy living support
- Relationship building
- Real fun and rest
  (This is huge. It's a key to being productive)
- Connection to giving and receiving love
- Calm curiosity
- Clarity/discernment

This is an awesome place to hang out in both your personal and professional life. It's where you're conscious. It where you feel calm clear and connected. This is where your best stuff happens. If you're doing something that is having a huge positive impact in your life, chances are it's an activity from this zone. This is the place where great stuff gets done, and love is most freely given and received.

Stay here. It's your happy place.

Effective, proactive people spend most of their time in The Productive Zone. To spend less time in the other zones you need to tell yourself and other people "no."

To-Do List Makeover Tool #5— Saying No

Learning to say no is key to healing your relationship with time. When I first started practicing this, I felt like I needed the other person to understand and approve of the reasons I had to say no. I would saturate her with exaggerated and woeful tales. Then, I'd wait with bated breath for her to tell me I was still okay and that she would still like me, even if I said no. Often, we both felt like we needed a shower when I was done.

A Cleaner Formula for Saying No

So, I've developed a cleaner formula for saying no.

Someone asks you to do something.

Then, you ask yourself three questions:

1. Do you want to do it?_____

2. Does it connect to your values/passions/vision?_____

3. Does it fit in the available time you have right now?_____

If the answer to *any* two of these questions is no, then your answer is no. If the answer to one or two of the questions is yes, you have the option to say yes. But you are still completely free to say no.

Oprah has been credited with saying, "No can be a complete sentence."

Often, the asker appreciates a clear, concrete answer, even when the answer is no. No one wants a needy onslaught, reeking of insecurity, and that requires effort to make *you* feel better. Or, even worse, a *yes* that's laden with resentment and bitterness.

Still, just plain no doesn't always feel right. If you're like me and prefer a softer approach, try this useful sentence **"Thanks for thinking of me. I've seriously considered your request and I have to say no. Good luck finding the right person."**

A couple of years ago, I asked a friend to head up a school committee. Her response felt so clean: "Jill, I appreciate your hard work and how challenging it can be to find people to fill these important volunteer commitments. I have decided not to take on this responsibility next year. I have confidence you'll find the right person for the job."

I felt empowered to move on and inspired to ask the next person. It was so much better than the "I can't *believe* you asked me" energy of some responses. It also felt much better than the "I'll just bury my head in the sand and hope she goes away" avoidance from others.

My friend showed compassion for my goals, but set a clear boundary with her available time. You can do it, too. As more than one life coach has been known to say, "Saying no makes room for a lot more yeses in your life."

Chapter 3

To-Do List Makeover
Part Two

These remaining to-do list makeover tools are going to stretch some of you. They require you to stop beating your-self up. So, your inner dictator, that mean voice in your head, may be very threatened. These tools will bring the story that "all *work* and no *play* makes Jack a worthwhile human" into question. So, take a deep breath, and open your mind.

To-Do List Makeover Tool #6—
"Choose to" vs. "Have to"

Even though very few of us write *"Have*-To-Do" on the top of our list, it's often what we're thinking.

"I *have* to cook dinner."

"I *have* to pick up my kids."

"I *have* to clean the house."

"I *have* to go to work."

But, that's not really true. I don't *have* to do anything but breathe today. Everything else I'm doing is a choice.

"But, but, but…" you may be saying, "The first three things on your example, I'll give you. Those may be choices. But I *have* to go to work, or I'll lose my job, and then I won't have enough money to pay my mortgage, and then I'll lose my house." That does not feel like a choice.

In reality, you *choose* to go to work because you don't like the potential consequences of losing your job, like not having enough money to pay the mortgage. It is still a choice. You are choosing to go to work to avoid the consequences that would occur if you don't go. It's a perfectly good choice. But it's important to recognize that it is still a choice.

Believe me, I have been a *slooowwwww* convert in this arena. When I first learned the theory that this language shift creates a significant motivation and perspective shift, this sometimes cynical old reporter was skeptical, to say the least. Still, I reluctantly agreed to test it out.

Choose-To-Do

To my surprise, when I wrote "Choose-To-Do" on the top of my list, I immediately felt a sense of relief. I connected to my power to make decisions, instead of the helpless, trapped, powerlessness I felt when I believed I *had* to do something.

When I tell myself I have to do something, my body jumps right into fight or flight mode. I'm like an animal in a cage, under threat, trying to stay safe. When I shift my thinking to recognize I have choices, it feels entirely different. I remain calmer, clearer, and more connected to solutions and creative ideas.

Just as I was letting that revelation sink in, one of my coaches (it takes a village) assigned me a new task. Instead of just writing "Choose-To-Do List" at the top of my list, she asked me to write "Get-To-Do List" at the top of the page.

"Oh, come on," I said.

However, I have always been a good student. So I followed directions, and took some notes to document what happened.

Get-To-Do List

1. Go to Grocery store – *Interesting. My inner dialogue shifts when I "get" to go to the grocery store, vs. "having" to go. I feel lucky to have three terrific stores within a mile of my house. I noticed I have enough money in the bank to pay for all we need. There's more on the shelves at one of these stores than is available to entire communities in most third world nations.*

2. **Fill out forms for lacrosse** – *Here, I connected to a love and appreciation for my daughter, instead of my usual low-level resentment about what this sports commitment would mean for my schedule, and mild angst about how she'll perform once she starts playing. It was so refreshing to feel nothing but peace and connection to exactly where she is right now, remembering how quickly these stages pass.*

3. **Finish presentation notes** – *This was interesting. "Getting" to prepare my presentation felt more playful and calm than "having" to do it. I immediately dropped the angst and need to impress that plagues my presentation preparation at times.*

Get-To-Do Worksheet

Pick 3 items on your to-do list right now.

#1.

#2.

#3.

How do you feel when you GET to do them?

#1.

#2.

#3.

Getting to Gratitude

Melissa, a mom of three children under the age of five and stepmom to a teenager, shared this story at one of my presentations. One morning, while describing the mountain of laundry that needed washing, she told her husband, "I can't ever get past all of it."

Melissa's husband (and many of us wives would agree he was treading on touchy territory here) gently reminded her that she wouldn't be folding tiny outfits for long. Rather than getting mad, her husband's observation connected to something powerful for Melissa.

"The next time I sat down to fold laundry, it clicked for me. You *get* to fold the baby's clothes. They are tiny little beings. They won't be in these for long. We are older parents. We watched my stepdaughter go from four to fourteen in an instant."

Melissa says that simple shift in thinking from exasperation to gratitude completely transformed one of her least favorite tasks. "Now, it makes me feel connected to my kids. I've turned folding laundry into a nice time for me."

My friend, the brilliant Sarah Seidelmann, M.D., is an author and expert on connecting people to the mystical gifts and guidance that nature can bring to our lives. She says, "Appreciation puts you in to a high state of FEEL GOOD and that's the place where you can let all the good stuff you want come to you."

This is important to understand.

Your brain is *unable* to feel gratitude and fear at the same time.

Connecting to gratitude in any situation is one of the best ways to activate your highest functioning, most discerning, efficient, productive self. Beginning to play with this concept, even in small doses, can reap huge rewards.

For now, remember, you are incapable of feeling fear and gratitude at the same time. Choose gratitude, and panic will dissolve.

After a seminar where I shared this tool, a recently downsized communications executive told me, "That is powerful! As I find myself in an unexpected (and arguably undeserved) career transition, I am remembering that I can't feel fear and gratitude at the time same. I have much to feel gratitude for, and it comes easily for me. Feeling gratitude instead of fear is refreshing, fun, and energizing. I am ready for my opportunity!"

To-Do List Makeover Tool #7— Put It on God's List

Part of this process is giving up the delusion of control with things in your life where you truly have no control.

When she experienced a stretch of overwhelm, author Esther Hicks decided to only put a few tasks that she could easily accomplish on a given day on her to-do list. Then she placed the rest of the items on another list that is for God (the universe, Jesus, the divine, or whatever you'd like to call it) to complete. She discovered *lots* of things could get done without her.

Here's one of my favorite examples of this:

My friend Miranda had a perplexing situation involving her horse, Sweetie.

After owning Sweetie for a year, it became clear the horse needed more training for her to be safe to ride. Miranda agonized over what to do next.

Should she sell her? To whom? Would she be able to recover the money she'd invested in the horse? Would Sweetie get the love and care she needed? Miranda couldn't stop fruitlessly fretting over "what if" scenarios and the "best" solutions. It was exhausting. So, she decided to let the matter rest for a little while. She chose to take it off her to-do list, and put it on God's list.

Not long after, out of the blue, a buyer came forward for Sweetie. Turns out this woman had experience training horses and was thrilled with the opportunity to work with Sweetie. As a matter of fact, the buyer had been through some tough times, and working with horses was a part of her plan for continued healing. To top it off, Miranda was welcome to visit Sweetie whenever she pleased.

Miranda's take? "It feels great to look back on the whole thing now and realize how everything came together in an amazingly wonderful way. What an unfolding of miracles! Wow."

Off My List

In the past, I've worried and toiled about getting this done: _____

_____

When I let it go, this happened: _____

_____

Things I'm worrying about right now: _____

_____

Is it in my control? _____

If the answer is "no", then put it on God's list:

If the answer is "yes," then follow previous steps of the

To-Do list makeover and see if it belongs on your calendar or To-Do list.

Other things that are on my To-Do list that are out of my control and belong on God's list: _____

_____

_____

_____

To-Do List Makeover Tool #8— The Fun Prescription

A big reason a lot of us have a hard time getting stuff done? Our inner dictator tells us it's all about productivity—that work needs to be constant and intense, or it doesn't count. "There's no time to for rest or frivolity, darn it!" it barks.

Ugh. Just writing that makes me want to go eat a box of donuts and play computer solitaire for six hours—anything to avoid the never-ending mean voice in my head. Here are some of her favorite lines:

"Fine, that's done, but you have so much more to accomplish."

"You can't sit down, you have too much to do."

"The work is never going to be done."

"You should have taken care of this earlier."

"Blah, blah, blah, blah….kvetch, kvetch, kvetch."

The truth is, in order to get more efficient and productive, you have to schedule in breaks throughout your day. I am easing you into this so your inner Gestapo officer doesn't blow an artery. But, *actually*, you don't just need to take a break, you need to make time for some fun.

Most people who find themselves overwhelmed are not avoiding tasks by engaging in a wacky fun activity. Usually, we're hiding out in the procrastination zone doing something mindless like computer games, junk TV, hours of perusing Facebook pages of people we haven't seen or cared about in 20 years, or other pretend busyness, all in order to keep from hearing our inner critic beat us up.

That's why, on my to-do list, I have a place for you to list something fun for you to do, and it's NOT after you have completed the entire list (see my template on page 52 at the end of this chapter.)

It doesn't have to be hours and hours of wild and crazy mayhem. It can be three deep breaths right after popping a piece of wintergreen gum, if that's what trips your trigger. But you need to be conscious and intentional—even determined—to make some time for fun.

Notice, the slot for fun is not for when you are *done* with everything. You don't have to wait until you're finished in order to "deserve" something fun. Creating time for fun is like refilling your gas tank.

It refuels you to accomplish.

Calendar Your Fun

Every single day put some time for yourself on your to-do list, or, better yet, on your calendar. It can be two minutes or ten hours. Pick an amount of time and a time of day that feels good to you. Make sure you treat that time as sacred and honor this commitment to yourself every single day.

I try to do something that I can **only** do in the particular season of the year that's happening right now. Some examples?

- Floating on a raft in the pool.
- Lounging on my backyard hammock.
- Waterskiing.
- Walking in the woods at sunrise.
- Riding horses with my friend.
- Standing barefoot outside.
- Drinking a giant mug of tea by the fire.
- Perusing catalogues for seasonal stuff.
- Making snow angels.
- Snow skiing.
- Taking drives to see the leaves changing color.

- Pinching off herbs in my little garden and smelling them.

Other things I like to do for fun breaks?

- Watch 2 or 3 funny videos on YouTube.
- Read a great book.
- Go to my favorite yoga class.
- Organize a closet (don't judge).
- Stand on my head (I said don't judge).
- Take a hot bath.
- Play "Words With Friends" with my sisters and parents who live out of state.

The Proof

Still not buying it? In a groundbreaking study on women and time, Real Simple magazine (April 2012) discovered that "…women who set aside free time on a regular basis, even though they had not finished all their chores, were happier, more cheerful, and more optimistic."

In addition, in a now-famous study at Northwestern University, researchers discovered participants who watched a funny movie did better on word puzzles than those who'd watched a horror film or listened to a science lecture. Light-heartedness can make us better problem solvers.

Not long ago, I was slogging through a nasty bout of writer's block. I had all these ideas, and couldn't quite figure out how I wanted to see them land on paper. I had to take a break to go pick up my daughter from driver's ed. She has been gifted with a wicked wit and was in a particularly silly mode that day. So, we started joking around on the way home. Before long, I was full-on belly laughing.

When I came home and sat down to write, I had a "Eureka!" moment and ideas and solutions came flowing out of me.

Fun/Funny = flow for me. As Martha Beck says, "Having fun is not a diversion from a successful life; it is the pathway to it."

Add Your Own Fun Prescription:

_____

_____

_____

_____

And sometimes you need to take a break from everything…even the fun stuff.

To-Do List Makeover Tool #9—Rest

Not long ago, I was having one of those *not enough time* nightmare days. I jumped on the metaphorical treadmill in the morning (it was already going too fast to be enjoyable) and it sped up all day to a pace that left me breathless.

I had not stopped moving all day.

Yet nothing seemed to be getting done.

So, late in the afternoon, when I finally noticed I had frenzied myself into a tornado of non-stop *un-productivity*, I did something crazy. I stopped. I took a deep breath. Then I listened to my body for just a microsecond. It said, "Rest." Loud and clear. *Rest.*

"What?????" My fear brain screamed. "There's NOOOOOOOO time!!!!!" But, fortunately, I am *onto* my fear brain. I know how it likes to show me "evidence" of how there's "not enough." But, when I look to my body for answers, it doesn't lie.

So, I went into my room and shut the door. I lay down on my bed. I felt a little panicky, afraid of what I was about to do. I just started taking deep breaths. Then, I thought of all the things I was grateful for in that moment.

My eyes welled up as I realized how much I appreciated the love I was showing myself. I connected to gratitude I felt for my bed, for my breath, and for my kids (who were leaving me alone). I felt the presence of the divine in that space. I let myself drift. I had 30 minutes of floating bliss.

I managed to hang on to that peace as I prepared dinner. I noticed time seemed to slow down. My monkey mind that had been jumping all over the place? It quieted down. My priorities got clearer. I didn't feel the panicked urgency. And I got some important stuff finished.

I know rest and meditation are a good idea. I just never had time. But now I know the real secret. Rest creates *more* time.

My nap story resonated with my old friend Marilyn. "Except," she said, "I kept plowing through the non-productivity. I ALMOST took a nap, and definitely should have listened to my body. Why do we get into those frenzies, and why don't we give ourselves permission to unplug, if only for a moment? Better late than never. Next time, I'll do the nap!"

My client Betsey, in the midst of running the family business, caring for an ailing loved one, holding a major volunteer leadership position, and planning her son's Bar Mitzvah, discovered naps were the key to getting stuff done. "Every time I felt overwhelmed, I knew I needed to rest. I kept a notebook by my bed. I came up with so many ideas when I let myself shut down. It was awesome."

Mastin Kipp, who visits me in my e-mail box every day in his wildly popular and unbelievably powerful blog "The Daily Love," said, "Rest is a part of making things happen. If we run ourselves too thin, we end up getting sick and injuring our body—which is not a long-term sustainable way to live. So, if you are crazy like me and are just GO GO GO and you are feeling the need to rest, how can you take a moment and let go, knowing that being in that space is the perfect thing for you to do to help you accomplish long-term?"

Reboot

Ever tried to use a computer when it's bogged down processing too much information? It's slow, inefficient, and wildly frustrating. The only way to get it running right again? Reboot. Your mind also needs breaks to reboot. Your body is a terrific barometer. When it feels tired, it means your brain needs a break, too. Listen to it.

Reboot. Do it with fun or rest.

Can't lie down and take a nap? Shut your door, turn off everything but classical or jazz music, close your eyes and breathe ten deep, slow breaths. Repeat three times.

Or, get up and move for a couple of minutes. Getting outside is a fabulous way to reboot. Taking a walk can be a powerful way to recharge.

"Anytime I find myself losing focus or I'm stuck in a particular way of thinking, I take a break and either take a walk or a shower. Almost every time, whatever I've been stuck on gets unhooked while I move my body or feel the hot water, and I get an insight or new idea that clears the path. When

I sit back down to my desk, I'm re-energized and can keep moving forward," says my friend, coach, and mojo-maker Kristin Stevens.

Another favorite way for me to reboot? I turn on my favorite dance music (80s music is my preferred genre for this) and dance like a banshee.

How do you know if you need to reboot?

Reboot Quiz

Do you find yourself dragging? _____

(if the answer is YES, see option "A" below)

Are you having trouble focusing? _____

(if the answer is YES, see option "B", below)

Are you finding everything/everyone annoying right now? _____

(if the answer is YES, see option "C", below)

Are you constantly daydreaming about how "everything would be better, if only…? _____
_____

(if the answer is YES, see option "D", below)

OPTION "A"--- You need to reboot.

OPTION "B"--- You need to reboot.

OPTION "C"--- You need to reboot.

OPTION "D"--- You need to reboot.

To-Do List Makeover Tool #10—S.T.O.P.

The final step in your to do list makeover? Know when to stop. At some point every day, we need to stop being the master of to-do's, and start being the master of done.

Wrapping It Up

Some of my clients like to create their to-do lists in the evenings for the next day. I like to do mine first thing in the morning. Either way, take a deep breath. Then another. Then, connect to what it is you really would like to accomplish in the actual time you have available.

Leave space. Recognize the creative, peaceful energy that helps you be your best is not squeezed out of tightly-packed, no-breathing-room schedules. Intentionally make time for soul-renewing stuff like fun and rest.

"It HAS to be done now!!!" is a panic-inducing lie my fear-brain loves to repeat. It's not true.

I get to choose.

To-do lists are just a way to help create the life you want. They can help you move from the self-flagellation of your inner critic into external support. Your to-do list is a container to hold the tasks that bang around in your head, making you feel inadequate, scattered, and disconnected.

Trust it to hold your stuff, and then make an effort to connect to the things you love and want to appreciate and don't let them pass you by. You *do* have time to stop and play with your kids. You *do* have time for another hug, or a discussion about how J.K. Rowling might describe that tree, or silly dancing in the kitchen.

No matter how terrific you become at creating to-do lists and crossing thing off your lists, if you still believe the thought *there's not enough time*, you will feel stressed. As a matter of fact, you may feel even worse if you are constantly working to get things done and you still fear you don't have enough time.

It's not your fault. It's a brain thing.

Let's take a look at why we're wired for time sabotage.

Get To-Do List

To-Do (Today)

1. _____

2. _____

3. _____

      Fun

      Rest

4. _____

5. _____

2-Minute Tasks (set your timer!!!)

1. _____

2. _____

3. _____

4. _____

5. _____

(Visit www.JillFarmerCoaching.com for a printable version of this page.)

Chapter 4

The Big Lie

I believe I have tried just about every trick and time management system out there. Many led me toward better organization and helped me develop habits to simplify. In my never-ending quest, I've come across some good ideas. At times, I would even get glimpses of calm.

Then, life would get busy again. Things would start to go awry. Before long, I'd be back to being overwhelmed. First, I would blame the system.

"It was too complicated."

"It didn't fit my personality."

"It was too rigid."

"It was too lax."

Next, I would blame myself for failing, once again, to get fixed.

"You've got to get it together."

"Everyone else has perfect houses, perfect kids, volunteers for everything, and makes lots of money in satisfying careers."

"When are you going to get it together?"

And, my favorite:

"You suck."

I was off the wagon, so to speak, letting things pile up, feeling like crap for not being able to get my act together, and on a procrastination and/or frenzy bender. I treated time like I treated most of my diets. I was either being good, or I was worthless, looking for the next new shiny program to make me better. After a while, it became clear that my addiction to time management systems was managing me.

I never seemed to be completely at peace—or feeling any peace, for that matter. No matter what I tried, I could *not* seem to be efficient enough to have sufficient time.

It didn't matter if I was preparing a live report on site hours after the Oklahoma City bombing for network television, or sitting outside on a beautiful day drawing with sidewalk chalk with my girls, I had a constant ticker running through my mind.

"I don't have enough time."

"I need more time."

"I'm too busy."

"There's too much to do."

"It never ends."

I was like a jukebox that could only find one painful playlist.

I never considered these as opinions, perceptions, or thoughts. They felt like facts. The truth. Indisputable observations. They circled around and around and around in my brain like an out-of-control merry-go-round. My constant complaining did nothing to change the situation. It was like I was trying to slow down the out-of-control ride by waving my hands in the air. It didn't work. Instead, I would just fall off of my metaphorical wooden horse and watch everything spin faster.

Little did I know the culprit for my out-of-control ride was all in my head. The never-ending time shortage story I kept telling myself launched a vortex that sucked me in, leaving me dizzy, disoriented, and desperate for a time fix.

Until I put the brakes on a very old pattern of thinking, no efficiency program, organizational plan, or time management system I adopted would make things better. The source of my woes was well hidden in my subconscious.

It could be lurking in yours, too.

Our Internal Software Glitch

To understand how we unconsciously let vast amounts of our time leak out of our life, it helps to understand a little about the brain; specifically, a part of the brain I hadn't thought much about since my last high school Anatomy and Physiology quiz back in 1987.

I'm not a neuroscientist (and I never played one on TV). So, I'll keep it simple (for my sake, not yours). The amygdala (ah-MIG-duh-luh) is a part of the limbic system in our brain. Among other things, it sends us warning/danger signals. It's the size of a peanut and shaped like an almond. No coincidence, since this tiny bundle of neurons can drive us all so nuts. It's part of a larger, primitive part of our mind that is responsible for a lot of our reactions.

Some experts call this our reptile brain or lizard brain because it is a not-so-evolved part of our nervous system. If you happen to be standing under a massive boulder, and you look up and notice it's tipping in your direction, your reptile brain's intense warning—complete with pounding heart, sweaty palms, jacked up blood pressure, and adrenaline surges—sends the message that you need to move, *now*.

You may be saying, "Thank you lizard brain, for keeping me safe."

Here's the problem: We get frightening "Beware! Your safety is at risk!" signals all the time, even when our lives are not *really* in danger.

Dr. Brent Atkinson says our primitive brains make snap judgments based on emotional memory. "Stress seems to increase the functioning of the amygdala, kicking it into overdrive."

Fight or Flight

That overdrive means we are in fight or flight mode (otherwise known as "hyperarousal") in which our stress hormones are raging and we're on edge, ready to react to the next possible danger.

Positive Psychology expert Gretchen Pisano puts it this way, "We're wired to scan our environment for threats."

"The entire purpose of your primitive brain is to continually broadcast survival fears—alarm reactions that keep animals alive in the wild," explains Martha Beck. "Our reptile brains are convinced that we lack everything we need: we don't have enough time, money, everything."

Not having enough time is hardly a life or death issue (unless you are MacGyver. Then, you only have 15 seconds before the whole nuclear power plant is going to BLOW.) Yet, our fear brain processes our lack of time as a threat to our survival. Why?

Neuroscientists tell us that when we're in fight or flight mode, it overwhelms logic and judgment. We react without the highest-functioning part of our brain being engaged at all.

My favorite name for this phenomenon is cranial abduction. Experts like Dr. Atkinson call it amygdala hijack. When our brain tells us we lack something, we literally react without thinking.

Again, when you are about to be hit by a speeding car and you jump out of its path with a split second to spare, *reacting without thinking* can be a good thing.

The rest of the time?

It's not so helpful.

Reacting without thinking is most certainly *not* the path to productivity, efficiency or peace.

Reacting vs. Responding

Let's spend just a minute talking about the difference between reacting and responding. Most of us use these terms interchangeably. But, for our purposes, they have pretty different meanings.

Reacting is automatic. Responding requires more forethought. For instance, when my kids are whining at me, I *react* by getting really mad, yelling at them, telling them they are driving me crazy, and threatening to ground them until the next millennium. In contrast, I *respond* to their whining by simply asking them if they will please use a different tone of voice. Or I tell them I'm going to the coffee shop to work and they will be fixing their own lunch today. Reacting is arbitrary. Responding is thoughtful. Reacting costs us time. Responding allows us to get more done.

One of my favorite examples to illustrate reacting vs. responding? My friend, Ali, an M.D. and a recognized researcher in her field, felt a monstrous time crunch on the morning of a huge grant presentation. Not long into her uber hectic morning, the intense "I need more time!!!!" thoughts pounded into a doozy of a headache.

She rushed into the medicine cabinet to grab some ibuprofen, being pelted with *not enough time* thoughts all the while. Not long after she swallowed the pills, Ali started feeling a little woozy. Turns out, in her fear-brain seized state, she'd *reacted* by grabbing the nighttime cold medicine (extra strength version), instead of the intended ibuprofen. That reaction cost her a loss of *time*, focus, and opportunity on a really important day.

When Rhonda, a corporate lawyer, returned home after a particularly arduous day at office, her 3rd grader ran up, waving a piece of paper. "Mommy, Miss Wilson says it's our turn to volunteer, since we haven't done anything to help all year."

(Guilt much, Miss Wilson? Sorry, I digress.)

Rhonda's son went on to explain he *had* to bring the makings of Daniel Boone Stew to school the next day. Rhonda had no idea what the hell was in Daniel Boone Stew, but she was fairly sure it didn't include the yogurt, expired horseradish sauce, and chardonnay that she currently had in her fridge.

Rhonda trudged off to the store, thinking "I don't have time for this!" all the way there. Once she arrived at the supermarket, she discovered she'd forgotten the ingredient list, *and* she'd left her phone on the kitchen counter. Thanks to her time shortage mindset, she couldn't recall one single item required for Daniel Boone stew.

So, feeling even more annoyed than when she'd first embarked on the errand, Rhonda raced home, and returned to the store with the list *and* her phone in hand.

However, this time she'd forgotten her wallet.

On her third trip back to the store, Rhonda only got as far as her car before she realized she'd left her cart of bagged groceries by the checkout lane.

Looking back, both Ali and Rhonda understand that their lack-based thoughts hijacked their best efforts and took over their abilities to think, reason, and problem solve. In both cases, their reptile reactions caused mistakes that ate up ginormous amounts of precious time.

Now, it's your turn. Take a minute to recall any instances where you reacted instead of responding.

Examples where my lizard mind has caused a reaction that cost me time.

1. _____

2. _____

3. _____

Fixed vs. Growth Mindset

When we are in that fight-or-flight, not-enough-time mode, we are extremely good at piling up evidence why things will never change, and why we will likely be stuck in our time shortage spin cycle until the dawn of eternity.

Researcher and author Carol Dweck (and others) call this a fixed mindset. It's that place where our mind takes on a stubborn stance. It processes every obstacle as an impenetrable roadblock, every challenge as a personal affront, and every required effort as a waste of irreplaceable energy reserves.

On the other hand, when we are able to tap into a growth mindset (more on that in Chapter 5), we look at obstacles as opportunities for growth, challenges as refinement experiences, and effort as the chance to get stronger.

When we are in a growth mindset, we look for possibility. When we are in a fixed mindset, we obsess over the problem. We react to every event with a "See, this is more proof things are never going to change," instead of, "Here's a chance to make things better."

I like to say a growth mindset makes us great at problem solving. A fixed mindset makes us great at problem *stalling*.

Listen to Your Body

A good way to tell if you are reacting versus responding is to take a couple of deep breaths and notice what you feel in your body when you think the thought *there's not enough time*.

Here are some examples of what reacting to that thought may feel like:

- Increased heart rate
- Tightness/tension in your muscles (I feel it most intensely in my shoulders and neck.)
- Knots in your stomach.
- Roiling or burning in your gut.
- Intense sensations in your solar plexus (right below the center of your rib cage).
- Sweating/flushing, feeling hot.
- Clenched palms or curled toes.

When you learn to notice where you feel your reaction in your body, you will begin to be able to short circuit the automatic sabotage that happens as a direct result of believing *there's not enough time.*

Not Good Enough?

Telling ourselves we don't have enough time is often joined by another unhelpful thought that stealthily sabotages our clock: believing we are not good enough. Even a low-grade sense of inadequacy creates another hidden hornets' nest of painful thoughts that can cost us countless hours.

A couple of years ago, my colleague and friend Kristin Stevens gently shared some hesitations she had about the title of this book. She found it jarring and thought it might turn people off. After all, is "There's Not Enough Time…" really a lie?

It sure felt like truth in her life.

When it came to taking care of her house, the kids, and domestic duties in general, Kristin could never seem to get it all done. This left her feeling inadequate, overwhelmed, and like an underachiever; all pretty unpleasant feelings for someone with a successful background in business, academics, and coaching.

Kristin revealed that deep down she believed she would never be as good as the ideal homemaker, her mother. Like many stay-at-home moms of her generation, Kristin's mom had cooked, sewed, organized, scrubbed, and polished her house and family with super-human prowess. Kristin didn't believe she measured up. How did this perceived inadequacy, this fear of not being good enough, cost her time?

Not good enough thoughts are fabulous time gobblers. They use two powerful methods to keep us feeling bad:

1. **They paralyze.** We begin to believe it's a losing battle anyway, so why bother? We feel so overwhelmed and unable to ever achieve the ideal that we are at a loss to take even one step toward the "impossible."

   Or,

2. **They propel** us into frantic, frenetic, panicky, constant motion. We need to look busy so we feel like we're worthwhile and to have any hope of measuring up to our creation of the ideal.

Neither of the above methods are models of motivation and efficiency. Believing we will never be good enough dwindles our precious energy reserves.

As we talked more about it, Kristin had a light bulb moment. She realized that continuing to try to relentlessly achieve her imaginary ideal would not make her happy, *at all.* So, we tried replacing the thought "I'll never be good enough" with a new idea that felt truer and better than the old one.

First, Kristin connected to what she really wanted in her home and family life. Was it to sew? No. She hates sewing. Was it to have a perfect-looking house at all hours of the day? No. And as it turned out, Kristin's husband and children didn't expect or want any of the items on her hidden ideal list. They wanted her to be peaceful, happy, and engaged with them. They wanted her presence. So her new thought became, "When I connect to love, the *right* stuff gets done." That helped Kristin prioritize things in a way that felt far less overwhelming or frenzied.

No more beating herself up for failing to achieve something that was incredibly distant from her authentic, essential self and that didn't connect with the heart or soul of her family goals. Instead, Kristin awakened a renewed focus toward connection and authenticity.

Now she helps other women find their purpose and harvest their mojo. To me, that's a *far* better way to use her time than beating herself up.

Better?

According to a doctor friend of mine, there's a saying in cardiology: "Better is the enemy of good." Here's my layperson's understanding of this concept: When a heart doctor gets 80% clearance of an arterial blockage in a cardiac catheter procedure, sometimes it's tempting to go back in to clear the remaining 20%.

Only that attempt at perfection can cause the blood vessel to blow, creating a life-threatening situation that could have been avoided if the doctor had accepted that 80% clearance of a blockage is, indeed, good enough.

I recently tested a non-life-or-death version of this theory. Last June, I wrote and edited my monthly newsletter in about two hours. I decided it could have been better. So, I messed around with it for another two hours. In doubling the time I spent on it, had I doubled the quality? Not even close. I liked some of the changes, but, in reality, I had probably improved the quality by 10%, at most.

When Is Good Enough, Good Enough?

Let's start with something you may do that requires a lot of effort *(an example: Planning and preparing Thanksgiving Dinner.)*

How much effort does this require
(on a scale of 1 to 10)?

_____

How much time compared to other meals you make
(on a scale of 1 to 10)? _____

_____

Money (on a scale of 1 to 10)? _____

_____

If any of the above answers are at 8, 9, or 10, imagine if you cut it back to a 5, 6, or 7 rating.

What happens to your stress level? _____

What are some steps you can take to make it "good enough"?

1. _____
2. _____
3. _____

No matter what you get done every day or how many things you cross off your list, if you focus on all you didn't get done or how much more you should be doing, you will always feel a sense of apprehension, uneasiness, or even dread.

Many of us have gotten used to living our lives with that angst as our constant companion. I'd love for you to make a new friend…your clock.

Chapter 5

Time Recovery

If there's only one thing you take away from this book, I hope you understand how one measly little thought can drain time from your life like a giant hole in a bucket. This next chapter is about learning to plug that hole and reclaim the time that's been pouring out…wasted, lost, and serving no one.

There's not enough time.

Simple words. If you're like me, you say them, or a variation of them, multiple times a day. This simple phrase is also a classic amygdala-driven thought. It's a perfect example of our fear brain talking; lack-based thinking at its very best. As you remember from the last chapter, fear-driven thoughts cause us to react, to act without thinking.

At one of my seminars, I asked a group of female physicians how they feel when they think the thought *there's not enough time.*

Without missing a beat, they shouted out:

"Panicky."

"Frustrated."

"Perplexed."

"Annoyed."

"Overwhelmed."

"Tense."

"Confused."

"Out of control.

"Hopeless."

Next, I asked them, when they're feeling panicky, frustrated, perplexed, annoyed, overwhelmed, tense, confused, out of control, and hopeless, how do they behave or react?

"Bitchy. I'm short with people."

"Unfocused, scattered, and disorganized."

"I can't prioritize."

"Frenzied."

"I'm overwhelmed, paralyzed."

"I shut down."

It's interesting to note that being overwhelmed and paralyzed seem to be the *opposite* of being hurried and frenzied. One action mode is characterized by complete immobility and one is characterized by constant motion.

Still, the end result for both is the same. We don't get anything done.

I first discovered how often thoughts like *there's not enough time* subconsciously take us in the opposite direction we want to go when I read Brooke Castillo's book "Self Coaching 101." The questions I asked the physicians and the worksheet below are based loosely on Brooke's stellar method for discovering limiting beliefs and dissolving them.

The thought *there's not enough time* creates an unpleasant body reaction, and launches a host of crappy feelings, which propel us to act in a wildly *inefficient* and *unproductive* manner. By simply thinking this one measly thought, we're launching a time-eating vortex.

Worksheet

When I think the thought "There's not enough time,"
I feel… (give me at least three emotions, here. Mad?
Sad? Glad? Start from there.) _____

_____

When I feel the emotions above, how do I behave?
(How's your focus? Productivity? How do you treat
other people?) _____

_____

What do I get done when I act this way? _____

_____

Ding, ding, ding. I'm willing to bet the farm that by simply thinking the thought *there's not enough time,* you are
launching an automatic reaction cycle that creates unpleasant feelings, which are the catalyst for actions that take you in
the opposite direction from where you want to go.

Creativity coach Jill Winski says, "The thought, 'there isn't
enough' creates feelings of urgency, anxiety, sadness, and regret. In a nutshell, it's fear. Then we take desperate, urgent,
anxious actions based on these feelings. And, no matter what
results we get, they don't feel like enough, because all of these
results have, as their backdrop, the belief that there just isn't
enough. We've cycled right back into our original thought,
and it all continues. No matter what we have, no matter what

we've created, it isn't enough, because our belief is that there isn't enough."

Just thinking the thought *there's not enough time* is costing you enormous amounts of time. Some would call it scarcity thinking. By focusing on the *lack,* we spend all of our time gathering substantiation to prove we have a shortage of or are missing what we want the most.

My friend Susan Hyatt, in her book, "Create Your Own Luck," says, "If I entertain the thought, 'I don't have enough time,' and leave it unattended, it will create a sensation of anxiety in my chest. I will look at my planner over and over and lament over everything I have to do. I become cranky…ultimately, my day is far from productive. What I do get done only receives a fraction of the energy and passion inside of me."

Problem Stalling

When we are trapped in the *not enough time* cycle, our fear mind loves to line up evidence to confirm life is conspiring to rob us of time, and that there's no solution. I call it problem stalling.

It's important to understand this is not our fault. Fear-based thoughts cause us to function out of the most primitive part of our mind. Blood is literally being diverted from the higher-functioning part of our brain to our large muscles (so we can fight or flee to avoid impending danger). We can't just calmly problem solve when we are in this "fight or flight" mode.

Here's how it works.

FIGHT: We are frantically and frenetically moving. We're constantly and desperately doing, without making any meaningful progress.

Or,

FLIGHT: We are procrastinating, hiding out, fleeing from doing anything meaningful.

So, how do we break this cycle? How do we keep the thought *there's not enough time* from sabotaging our brain and siphoning off so many of our precious hours? You can short-circuit the vortex that sucks away so much of our time with a very simple step.

Notice

It is really that easy. By simply *noticing* you are having the *not enough time* thought, again, you take yourself from that primal, reactionary part of your brain where you act without thinking into the higher-functioning part of your mind.

Brain experts call it taking your thinking from the neural back alley to the forehead. Noticing takes you to a higher level of consciousness and awareness as opposed to that automatic hijacked brain mode.

Noticing allows you to snap out of the giant time suck. (See "The Happiness Trap" by Russ Harris for more on this phenomenon.) Again, it takes you from a mind state where you are problem *stalling* into one where you can problem *solve*.

Tips for Noticing:

1. Simply say to yourself, "I notice I'm having the *there's not enough time* thought again."
2. Touch two fingers to your lips and take three deep breaths (for more awesome ideas on disrupting stress circuits, read "Buddha's Brain" by Rick Hanson & Richard Mendius)
3. Connect to the present. Take a look around. Notice your surroundings, check in with your body.

Additionally, remember what I said back in Chapter 3 about not being able to feel fear and gratitude at the same time? Consciously connecting to gratitude is a great restart button for your mind. Take a minute to list five things you are deeply and genuinely grateful for right now, and you will stop your reactions before they start spinning out of control, eating up your time.

Gratitude Tool

List 5 things you are deeply and genuinely grateful for in this moment. You need to genuinely *feel* gratitude. You can't just go through the motions.

1. _____

_____

2. _____

_____

3. _____

_____

4. _____

_____

5. _____

_____

A teacher friend caught herself teetering on the edge of panic right before the holidays. End-of-semester deadlines, grading, and projects had her incredibly busy at work. She hadn't even begun to tackle holiday cards, decorating, or gift buying. As she felt herself launching into a cyclone of pre-holiday stress induced destruction, she simply took a couple of deep breaths and said, "I notice I'm telling myself *there's not enough time.*"

Her husband looked at her like she'd had one too many eggnogs. But, she told me the effect was immediate. Just by consciously noticing the thought (a giant burning orb in her gut was her first clue) the precipice she *almost* jumped into closed up. She couldn't wait to tell me it worked.

The Three Cs

Effective time management requires discernment, clarity, and creativity, all things you can access when you are in a calm, clear, connected state. I call it the three C's.

1. Calm
2. Clear
3. Connected

We literally create new opportunities (not to mention new neural cells) when we cultivate the three C's. I refer to it as being in the zone. You may think of it as your sweet spot. Understanding how the thought *there's not enough time* holds you hostage and sabotages your best self is the first step. Noticing you're having the thought before it can suck you down the vortex is the next.

Once I finally figured out that being in "fight or flight" mode all of the time was making me a raging reactionary and that I was unwittingly setting off time bombs that wreaked unnecessary havoc at every turn, things miraculously started getting calmer.

And the granddaddy of all the ways to recapture giant chunks of time in your life is to replace the thought *there's not enough time* with a thought that will serve you instead.

How about, there *is* enough time?

What if there *is* enough time? What happens when you think *that* thought?

"Now, just wait a rabble-rousing minute," you may be saying. "I can't believe that thought. It just doesn't seem true."

During a session with a group of surgeons, a woman piped up, "I can't buy it. I *don't* have enough time!"

I gently reminded her that every thought is just a measly set of words that we attach with meaning. Then, I asked her how many hours there are in a day.

"24," she said with a quick head shake and an eye roll.

Next, I asked her if that amount was fixed or variable.

"Fixed, of course," she responded. Note: Really smart doctors don't like it when you question their scientific prowess with lame questions.

"So," I said. "If it's a fixed amount, the amount of time we have is non-negotiable. We all have the same 24 hours. If arguing against that realty isn't working so well, why not try something different?"

So, I asked the doctors at my seminar to take a deep breath and say "There IS enough time."

How did they feel?

"Calmer."

"Clearer."

"More relaxed."

"Relieved."

"More content."

"Motivated."

"Hopeful."

How do they behave when they are calmer, clearer, more relaxed, relieved, content, motivated, and hopeful?

"Focused. A lot more focused."

"Kinder."

"Efficient."

"More patient."

"More productive."

"I get more done!!"

Ding. Ding. Ding.

Just by thinking the thought there *is* enough time, we trigger a cycle that taps into our most efficient, productive selves. We give ourselves the gift of time.

As an added bonus, when we believe the thought *there is enough time*, we're empowered to stay present, and not drop below consciousness into the fear cycle that makes us feel so bad.

Worksheet

When I think the thought "there IS enough time," I feel…(give me at least three emotions/states of mind.)

_____

_____

_____

When I feel the emotions above, how do I act? (How's your focus? Productivity? How do you treat other people?) _____

_____

_____

What do I get done when I act this way? _____

_____

_____

Dana, a working mom, had somehow let the family vacation sneak up on her. Now, with less than an hour before she needed to leave for the airport, she raced around her home with the fury of the Tasmanian devil, only with less civility.

There was no way she could get everything packed in time to leave. She felt crazed. Somehow, despite the white noise crackling through her spasming brain, Dana heard a gentle voice in her head saying "There *is* enough time."

She repeated it to herself a few times.

"It was unbelievable. I got instantly calmer. Everything got really clear. I knew exactly what I needed, and where I needed to find it. I was hyper-focused," she said. "I felt directed. I even ended up having a few minutes to pick up the items I'd thrown around in my outburst. We made it to the airport with time to spare. I really couldn't believe it."

I can't tell you how many times people tell me stories of things miraculously falling into place, or things working out unbelievably well when they switch to this thought. Even some of the most cynical skeptics report back later that they gave it a try, and it worked!

The Negativity Bias

If you're like me, you've heard the term the negativity bias, but you may not be exactly sure what the experts mean by it, or what it has to do with the lack of time in your life. The negativity bias is a psychological phenomenon in which we pay more attention and give more importance to negative information and experiences than positive ones. It's why:

- We obsess over the two people who didn't come to our party instead of relishing in the joy experienced by the other 25.
- When we hear something negative and something positive about someone we don't know, we tend to remember the negative.
- We can hear a dozen compliments. But we ignore those as soon as a single criticism emerges.
- No matter what we're doing, we could really use more time. **We never have enough time.**

Our negativity bias lives in that primitive part of our mind we've been talking so much about. The good news?

Just by becoming aware, you can tap into the power of positivity, located in your pre-frontal cortex, where a whole lot more advanced brain power lives.

Acceptance vs. Resistance

Often, our time battles can be directly connected to our resistance. Specifically, our resistance to what is. Resistance doesn't change reality. It just makes life harder. It's like being really, really thirsty, then packing your glass with cotton balls before you take a drink of water. You may still get some liquid to dribble out—but it's hardly the quench you are craving.

Resistance takes great energy. It's also one of the most powerful God-blockers there is. But acceptance provides space for the divine. It births ideas and answers. I experienced this on a bike ride recently. The headwind that morning was far more powerful than I'd realized.

"This stinks."

"It's too much work."

"Why is the wind blowing so hard?"

Yada, yada, yada, blah, blah, blah, kvetch, kvetch, kvetch…

Once my mind got going, it took off, rolling through one negative (unhelpful) thought after another. After about 20 minutes (which felt like an hour) I turned around headed back, anticipating a healthy gust propelling me from behind. But I noticed the wind felt *a lot* stronger when we were riding into it than when it was at our back. The wind had created its own resistance, but my resistance to it made it so much worse. It made me wonder: How often do I take things that are kind of hard and resist them until they become intolerable, at least in my mind?

On the last leg of my ride, with the wind at my back, I discovered so many beautiful things: perfect bird nests camouflaged in the field, the symmetry of the waves in the river backwater, the budding trees on the ridgeline. All of this had been available to me on the first half of my ride. But I failed to see them. I was too busy resisting the wind. It made me wonder what else I'm missing in my life when I'm in resistance mode.

But, back to you.

Responsive Living

Remember, when you're in a calm, clear, connected brain state, you are more creative and better at strategic thinking. So, accept instead of resist whatever is going on in your day, and believe there *is* enough time before you create your to-do list—and your discernment abilities and efficiency will be at their best.

According to one of my favorite writers on the subject, Rick Hanson, science is really beginning to give us some answers that prove this. He says, "When the body is not *disturbed* by hunger, thirst, pain, or illness, and when the mind is not disturbed by threat, frustration, or rejection, then most people settle into their resting state, a sustainable equilibrium in which the body refuels and repairs itself and the mind feels peaceful, happy, and loving."

Hanson calls this our "responsive" mode of living. He goes on to say, "It is our home base, which is wonderful news. We are still engaged with the world, still participating with pleasure and passion, but on the basis of a background sense of safety, sufficiency, and connection."

We don't always get to choose what happens in our lives. But we can always choose how we respond to it. When you shift your thinking even a little, by beginning to believe there *is* enough time, you can slide into that responsive mode of living, where time is a gift, not an enemy. It's a place where opportunities abound, and problems cease to compound.

Don't get me wrong, I know you're still going to encounter tasks, jobs, and obligations that make you cringe or even want to hide. Never fear, I've got you covered. Read on.

Chapter 6

Motivation, Momentum, and Tackling Big Projects

The source for the dark cloud of shame that hung over Kinara's head? A basement stuffed to the gills with stored items and clutter. Mary Beth's dome of doom? The recertification required in her particular field of the medicine. For Jo, the sale of her deceased parents' home and all of its belongings created a hovering thunderhead of dread.

For each of these women, a big project stood smack dab in the way of their sense of adequacy or accomplishment. Based on the amount of energy it consumed, you'd assume these bright, loving, and competent ladies were toiling night and day, overwhelmed by the sheer volume of tasks associated with their particular big projects.

Nope.

See, these women hadn't started *doing* anything to

tackle these overwhelming jobs. The stories of how impossible each behemoth would be to complete just festered in their heads, sucking their mental energy dry. It produced a fog of despair that grew darker and more ominous with each passing day.

Visions of completing their projects were murky, at best. When they didn't feel dread, worry, or shame about slaying these legendary dragons, they felt just plain hopeless. They spent months doing nothing, feeling horrible all the while.

Why the wailing and gnashing of teeth about something they weren't even doing? Often, before we start a big project, our mind weaves dastardly and disturbing stories about how much effort and time and how many resources it will take. So, we stay frozen. Immobile. Guilty. Ashamed. Panicked. And completely unmotivated.

Getting Rolling

When we're overwhelmed, we have a tough time getting started. It's like we're telling ourselves we have a giant 300 pound orb (with a map of the world on it) that we need to pick up, heft onto our shoulders, and move from point "A" to point "B" while staggering under its debilitating weight. It sounds painful, unbelievably difficult, or even downright impossible.

No wonder it's hard to begin. When it comes to big projects, our job *isn't* to lift up this impossibly globe. Our job is to lean up against it. We just need to get the ball rolling, so its own weight can move it where it needs to go. Momentum creates ease where there's been effort. This whole chapter is about dissolving the roadblocks so we can get rolling.

Worksheet: Motivation—rolling into momentum

Project/task that's looming over my head right now:

_____

_____

_____

Why I haven't started it: _____

_____

_____

What about it feels overwhelming (or under-inspiring)?

_____

_____

_____

Why I'd like to get it done: _____

_____

The Why Foundation

If you take a look at the reason you want to complete this project, you'll get the clearest picture of the reason you're having trouble getting started. 90% of the time when I'm working with clients on accomplishing big projects, their "why" sounds something like this:

"Because I don't want to be embarrassed by the guest bedroom anymore."

"Because I don't want to miss out on my chance for promotion."

"Because I have let all this stuff pile up and should have dealt with it years ago."

"Because I don't want to be ashamed about my weight any longer."

Notice the pattern? Everyone is trying to motivate themselves from a place of what they *don't* want. I have watched clients go from dragging their feet for years to hopping into inspired action and completing their big project after making *one* simple change: They transform their *why*. (Author and speaker Simon Sinek has some amazing stuff on discovering and shifting your why. Check out his TED talk for some outstanding inspiration on discovering your purpose.)

Transforming Your Why

Motivation that comes from pain isn't really motivation. It is beating yourself up. It's another form of shoulding all over ourselves. It causes us to avoid. We busy ourselves with other, less meaningful tasks.

Shifting your why to something that encourages, supports, and expresses kindness and love fires up a completely different part of your mind, the part that is great at:

1. Problem solving

2. Resource gathering

3. Future planning

All the components that make getting big projects done a lot more likely. Here's how the "I don't wants…" from above converted their whys:

Why?

Before = *Because I don't want to be embarrassed by guest bedroom anymore.*

After = Because I love the idea of hosting friends and family in our home.

Why?

Before = *Because I don't want to miss out on my chance for promotion.*

After = Because I'm ready to enjoy new challenges and pursue new opportunities.

Why?

Before = *Because I have let all this stuff pile up and should have dealt with it years ago.*

After = Because I want other people to enjoy this stuff, if they'd like it, and I love how free and clear I feel when I create space in my home.

Why?

Before = *Because I don't want to be ashamed about my weight any longer.*

After = Because I'd like to live a long life full of vitality and energy.

Your "Before" = *Because* _____

_____

Your "After" = Because _____

_____

Amy Pearson, author of "I Don't Need Your Approval," says it more beautifully than I ever could: *"I used to take my goals very seriously. I used them as a measuring stick, a way to quantify my self-worth. I had a list of things I was supposed to accomplish by the age of 30. I was supposed to speak four languages, graduate with honors from Columbia University, solve the hunger problem, win the Nobel Peace Prize, etc., etc....*

As you can guess I fell short.

So the goals I created back then were really more like intangible torture devices. Each time I came up short, I used the goal to figuratively whack myself on the head.

Nine years later, there's a different energy behind my goals. The stakes are not so high—yet, ironically, I'm achieving my goals more often and I'm much happier.

Part of it has to do with permission. I now give myself permission to just be happy. Not happy "if." Not happy "when." The by-product, I have found, is that when I can Just. Be. Happy. I don't judge what I want as stupid, frivolous, or just plain crazy. And my goals get to be for me not about me.

Second, I am way more willing to fail than I used to be. Since my goals are now my source of joy—a gift I give to myself, really—and not a measuring stick with which to beat myself over the head, I can afford to be creative, daring, and at times downright cray-cray."

Before we launch into action and get going on creating a plan to get your big project tackled, we need to address the two P's that will always get in the way of achieving your big project goals: procrastination and perfectionism.

Procrastination

"Procrastination doesn't count as down time," says my friend Linda Bucher, Master Life Coach. So true. Procrastination is not resting. It's not rejuvenating. It's not rebooting. It douses energy with regret and shame. Often, we don't consciously make the decision to procrastinate. It sneaks up on us and sabotages.

I love how my friend Shirley categorizes procrastination. "It comes in through the back door and distracts and paralyzes me, keeping me from getting my big project done." Procrastination is not empowering. It's an unwanted guest. It's also usually not something we consciously choose. So, it takes a little curious and compassionate inquiry to notice how you're holding yourself back.

1. How do you procrastinate?

Do you hide out surfing the internet? Do you launch into busywork? Do you make yourself available at all hours of the day and night to distractions from others? Simply notice the sneaky, hiding out tricks procrastination uses in your life, you can begin to make choices that serve you.

2. Do you need to rest or reboot?

Remember, as Neale Donald Walsch said, "...we are human *beings*, not human *doings*." Procrastination may just be a signal you're trying to do too much. You may need to consciously rest to refuel. Or, you may need to reboot with some powerful fun, or meaningful movement (a walk outside, some yoga, or other exercise that feeds your soul.)

3. Will delaying this project help?

Sometimes, there's a perfectly good reason to wait. When we recognize that, we are able to calm our angst and connect to patience. However, if delaying will *not* help, it's best to be honest with ourselves, reconnect to our why and start moving forward (I'll tell you how, shortly.)

Perfectionism

Listening to my buddy Kinara lament the disaster in her downstairs for the 142nd time (in 15 days), I gently and lovingly asked, "Why in the *hell* don't you just start on it, then?!?!"

"I can't even begin this project until I have a solid week to finish it," she responded.

Ah, the old chunk of time theory. Lots of my clients come to me with stories of how they would most certainly achieve their dreams, *if only* they had the proper chunk of time to do it. Most of the time, this magic chunk of time fails to materialize. When miracles do occur, and it does appear, we often fritter it away because it feels kind of sucky to do nothing during our time off but tackle a gigantic project that's haunted us for a long time. Kinara didn't want to spend her only vacation in two years working nonstop in her basement? What a shocker.

Of course, the chunk of time theory is really just perfectionism hiding in a powerful excuse. "It's going to take SOOOO long to do this job, *perfectly,* I might as well just give up, or keep procrastinating." It's really hard to get motivated when we have stories about how hard it's going to be and how perfect it needs to be when we're done.

If you find yourself telling chunk of time stories, go back

and review "good enough" at the end of chapter 4. Then, come back here and keep reading. I'm about to show you know to make your big project feel ridiculously easy.

Turtle Steps

We're about to learn my favorite solution for moving through the place we get stuck before we start on our big projects. It's called turtle steps (Martha Beck's term) breaking down big tasks into "ridiculously easy" smaller steps to get moving toward a goal.

Meet my favorite turtle friend, Saul. I am his trainer. You will soon see why my career in animal handling is likely going to be a short-lived job. I have set Saul down at point "A." I have instructed Saul to leap on over to point "B."

"Come on, boy," I plead.

After 45 minutes, he hasn't moved an inch. Saul peers at me with his soulful turtle eyes and says, "I'll never get there." Why is Saul stuck at his starting point? Well, it is physiologically impossible for him to *leap* ten feet to his destination. So, he feels overwhelmed, perplexed, and paralyzed.

After I remember Saul can't leap, a light bulb clicks on for me. Saul needs to let his short little legs propel him one step at a time. He needs to take turtle steps, the way God created him to move. When I instruct Saul to start turtle stepping, he gets those turtle legs rolling, and, in no time at all, he reaches his destination without breaking a sweat.

You, too, can tackle even the biggest projects, one turtle step at a time.

A Turtle Step Is:

1. **Ridiculously easy.** I mean *so* easy you can't help but do it.
2. **Ridiculously easy.** Such a small step that you're not even sure it counts. The smaller, the better.
3. **Ridiculously easy.** You feel no resistance.

The most important turtle step is the first one. For Marybeth, the doctor who wanted to get recertified, turtle step #1 was "Turn on computer." She laughed about it. But, it got her going. Two months later, she passed her tests with flying colors.

My favorite tweet from marketing guru Marie Forleo is, "Starting small doesn't mean thinking small." In other words, avoid telling yourself that doing small steps doesn't count.

Kinara's first turtle step? Looking up companies who rent dumpsters to see how much that would cost. It turned out to be cheaper than she thought, and throwing away tons of broken stuff (without the hassle of hauling it away herself) proved really convenient, and cleared space for her to sort the rest.

For Jo, who needed to liquidate her parents' belongings and sell their house, a first turtle step was calling friends who had already done this to ask for recommendations of auction companies. They shared invaluable resources that made the entire process go smoothly.

Jo, Kinara, and Marybeth all discovered that making even a tiny bit of headway propelled them into inspired action. In their book "The Progress Principle," authors Teresa Amabile and Steven Kramer say, "Real progress triggers positive emotions like satisfaction, gladness, even joy. It leads to a sense of accomplishment and self-worth." The authors say even small, incremental steps lead to greater creativity and productivity.

Plan It Out

Once you've come up with a ridiculously easy first step to get your globe rolling, it's time to create a plan to take your big project from start to finish. Your plan is going to consist of nothing but turtle steps. This plan can take different forms. I'm going to give you three different options that I've found work really well.

1. **Flow Chart Method** – You create a very simple flow chart to sequentially move you through your turtle steps to completion. Go to **www.TheresNotEnoughTime.com** for an example of a flow chart using turtle steps. There's also a template for you to create your own flow chart. Remember, it's really, really important that each step on the chart is ridiculously easy.

2. **List Method** – This is as simple as it sounds. Plan out your project with a list that lays out your turtle steps from start to finish. This method makes it particularly easy to transfer individual turtle steps to your daily Get-To-Do list.

3. **Sticky Note Method** – Put each turtle step on a sticky note and then put them in order on a blank piece of poster board or a wall. Some of my clients love the tactile experience of crumpling up the sticky note as they finish each individual turtle step.

Having a plan that lays out your steps from start to finish will do a few really important things:

#1. Often our scary stories make a big project seem a lot harder and more intimidating than it really is. I can't tell you how many clients say "That doesn't seem as difficult as I thought it would be" once they see their flowchart or list.

#2. Having the entire process mapped out makes it less likely you'll get lost and abandon ship halfway to your destination.

#3. Laying out the entire plan makes it easier to recruit or hire help. That way, you can give clear, concise directions for someone else to help you complete one set of turtle steps, while you work on another.

Business coach and marketing genius Laurie Foley has another great reason to lay out the project, "With bigger projects, the list helps me know the order of things and, increasingly in my business, how to replicate things so that I don't have to reinvent processes every time. This saves me tons of time."

One of my favorite friends, K.K., summed it up beautifully, "The chunk of time theory defines my thinking perfectly when it comes to getting tasks done, but I never knew how to describe it. In this crazy stage of life with little ones, it seems like not only was I waiting for a chunk of time to get something totally done, but I needed it to be a chunk of time either without the kids or while they're napping. Those hours of the day are certainly numbered! So, I love the idea of the turtle stepping, and have been putting that to the test the past two days. It's really helping! My kitchen was a complete disaster yesterday, and unfortunately I just kept letting it get worse and worse as it looked more overwhelming. But when I stopped to 'turtle step it' and first put up items in the pantry, then unload the kids' school dishes, etc., it actually got done in less time than I would have guessed."

Use Your Timer . . . Carefully

As I've said before, I'm a huge timer fan. (Time Timer is my favorite.) And, setting a timer can be a great place to start rolling with turtle steps. However, I'm not a huge fan of the highly rigid "on and off" timer methods of time management where you work for a specific amount of time, then rest for a specific amount of time and earn longer breaks when you've put in "enough" time.

When I've tried these methods, I end up chained to my timer, obsessed with whether I'm doing enough and driving myself back to work after my "rest," even when my body still needs a break. I find these methods a little draconian. To me, they are a lot like a diet: The structure is enticing, and they're easy to commit to, for about a nanosecond. Then, they provide evidence of my failure when I fall off the wagon or stop adhering to the rules.

Lovingly and gently using your timer on big projects can be very helpful, as long as you don't use it to flog or otherwise beat yourself up. Set your timer for a period of time that feels ridiculously easy for engaging in your big project. Again, avoid stories about what "counts" or what's "long enough." Just pick an amount of time that feels ridiculously easy. It may be five minutes. It may be an hour. That's up to you. When your dinger dings (that sounds kind of racy), take three breaths and decide if you're feeling *engaged* and *in the flow*, or whether you want to take a break for some fun, rest, or another kind of reboot.

Batching

When you use all of the tools from this chapter, dissolve your motivation/ momentum blockers, and get on a roll, "batching" (a productivity term for grouping similar tasks together) can also be really helpful. The theory behind it? When you've geared up to do a task, and you're focused on what it takes to get it done, it's easier to knock out a number of the same tasks at once.

Every day around 5 o'clock, I would try to psych myself up to decide what the heck we would have for dinner, and start the process of putting a meal on the table. It felt onerous, monumental, and mildly annoying just about every day that I had to come up with supper ideas and cook.

Then, I started batching our dinners. I surveyed the family and got ideas for dinner entrees for the week. I would buy the ingredients for a bunch of those entrees and spend one afternoon cooking the main courses for the next several days. I froze them so they could be easily reheated, for the simplest meal prep ever.

Instead of expending the mental energy to pick menu selections every day (not to mention the physical effort entailed in cooking and cleaning up) I batched it into one sitting. I did several days' worth of tasks and grouped them into one project.

You can use this tool for an infinite number of projects. Business coach Jenny Shih advises clients to write a few blog posts in one sitting. That way, instead of slogging through their writing chores and climbing "Mt. Writers' Block," every week-- only to traverse the same uphill trek a week later— they can knock out several weeks' worth of writing in one fell swoop.

Batching is not the opposite of turtle stepping. It's just

doing a bunch of turtle steps in one sitting, while you've got momentum rolling. It's really just another way to create ease. An artist friend finds when she tries to hop in and out of projects when she has a minute or two, it blocks her creative flow. So, she prefers to block out larger amounts of time to get deeply and fully engaged in what she's doing to make significant progress.

The bottom line: Check in with your body and emotions to see what feels best for you. If setting aside larger periods of time is possible and batching lots of steps in one project or multiple projects feels great to you, then do it.

E-Mail: Enemy #1 for Momentum

I find batching works beautifully with reading e-mails, as well. Rick, an executive client, came to me ready to hurl his desktop of out of his penthouse office. He could never seem to get anything done. Every time he tried to finish up a project, stay focused on a key phone call, or launch a new deal, the chime would ring on his computer, alerting him that another e-mail had arrived.

The distraction of e-mail derails focus, and it can take as long as 15 minutes to get fully reengaged again. I told Rick it was no wonder he didn't feel like he could get anywhere.

It was like he was flying in a plane—and every time he got an e-mail, he would have to land to deal with it. Landing and taking off every few minutes is not an efficient way to travel.

So, Rick started batching his e-mails and checking them once an hour, for 10 minutes. He couldn't believe how much more focused he felt. He found it a lot easier to complete projects, concentrate during phone calls, and come up with business expansion ideas. Also, instead of being constantly annoyed and resentful about the e-mails, he was able to be clear, concise, and more on target with his responses.

Here's my e-mail strategy. I've used it for a while, now. It's helped me successfully handle up to a couple hundred e-mails a day, with under 20 remaining in my inbox at a time.

Jill's E-mail strategy

I check e-mails once in the morning, and every 2-3 hours for the rest of the day. I set my timer and limit the amount of time I spend to about 10 minutes. Any responses that I can't get to in that amount of time, I put in a separate folder. I put 30 minutes on the calendar later in the day (or the next day) to tackle e-mails that require more time.

I have turned off the e-mail chime on my computer. That way, I'm not jumping off whatever I'm doing to constantly check new e-mails coming in.

I try not to check e-mail on my smartphone, because, when I do, I end up reading the same e-mails over and over (on my smartphone, tablet, and then desktop), and I can't seem to remember whether or not I've replied. Instead, I wait until I can get to my desktop.

A Whole New Definition of Overwhelm

Overwhelm, the biggest roadblock to our motivation and momentum, may just be the result of a misunderstanding. Lots of us treat being overwhelmed as a plague, a pox, a horrific affliction that threatens to swallow our entire being with its oozy, flesh eating, life-sucking infectious self.

In other words, we don't like it.

We frenzy ourselves into a tizzy to try to avoid it—which, of course, only makes things even worse.

What if you made overwhelm your friend?

Ouch. The incredulous scream in your head directed at me actually hurt my ears from the inside. What if you quit trying to hide from overwhelm? What if you greeted it as a messenger, a deliverer of some precious insight? What if overwhelm carried a gift for you?

Sarah Yost, founder of The Shiny Object School, says it beautifully:

"Overwhelm is a just signal you're doing too much. Overwhelm is a great thing. We act like overwhelm is terrible. Overwhelm is a wonderful signal to let you know that you're trying to do much at once and you need to back it up." She goes on to say, "It doesn't mean what you're trying to do is bad, just that there's something wrong with what's right there in front of you."

Chapter 7

Eliminating Dreaded Tasks

Even when you've figured out how to be motivated instead of blocked, and how to use momentum to make things easier, there are still things that come up on our to-do lists that we aren't so jazzed to complete. Cleaning toilets comes to mind.

I call them dreaded duties or DDs. They're not "have tos" (see the start of Chapter 3 for a refresher on this). We are *choosing* to do them. They're just those things we really don't always *want* to do. In addition to the aforementioned toilet tending, here are some other examples of DDs from my clients.

- Weeding the garden.
- Filling out forms of any kind.
- Taking young kids to get a haircut.
- Renewing a driver's license.
- Paying library fines.

- Anything to do with filing taxes.
- Going to parent/teacher conferences with an ex-husband and his new wife and her recently purchased fake boobs.
- Window washing.
- Writing handwritten Thank You notes.
- Grocery shopping.
- Buying a gift for the mother-in-law.
- Washing the car.
- Pelvic exams.
- Prostate biopsies.

Notice that when you look through this list some of the items make you moan and cringe, but others look like big fun. "Who doesn't LOVE a good window washing?" you may ask, incredulously. You may believe the department of motor vehicles is the best place to hang out and pass the time. Perhaps pelvic exams provide a bonding experience for you and your doctor.

Understand—one person's DD is another's nirvana. No judgment. It's only important you understand your *own* list of DDs, because it's likely they are tripping you up, slowing you down, or getting in the way of doing what you really want.

Your Dreaded Duties List

_____

_____

_____

_____

_____

_____

_____

_____

If you're not careful, DDs can bring momentum to a screeching halt. They lurk around the edges of our subconscious, irritating us. All piled up, DDs start to feel like a huge big project. Leave them lying there long enough, and they start to stink to high heaven. Unattended, DDs are major progress blockers.

The Three Bs

Martha Beck developed my favorite method for dissolving dreaded duties and tiresome tasks. It's called the "3 Bs." You can use it whenever you encounter something that causes you to pause, to feel disdain, or generally leaves you feeling like you'd rather hang from your toenails than just do it. It's actually a set of three questions you ask yourself every time you encounter a DD.

Should I…

1. Bag It?
2. Barter It?
3. Better It?

B #1= Bag It?

Do I really need to do this task? Or, do I really need to do it today?

Simple question. But sometimes we get so caught up in *accomplishing* something and crossing it off of our list, we forget to examine whether or not we really *need* to do it. Sometimes we do things just because we always have. Or, we do things just because we're afraid of what other people will think if we don't do it.

I shared the 3 Bs tool at a women's retreat I led. After I finished speaking, Jean, a spry 78-year-old, beelined right up to me: "Jill, that changed my life! I've figured out how to be less stressed," she said, triumphantly. Beaming with pride, I dared to ask what I had done to garner such praise.

"Why, it's those 3 Bs," she replied.

I asked which B had so powerfully impacted her.

"Bag it. I'm NEVER ironing sheets again," she said.

Given the level of her bliss at this revelation, I didn't feel it appropriate to let her know I'd never heard of ironing sheets. I didn't even know it could be done. There's really never been a lot of ironing of anything going on at my house. During one of my mom's visits, my young daughters beheld the sight of the strange contraptions identified as an iron and ironing board with wonder and amazement. They had never seen them.

Anyway, Jean simply asked herself the question, "Do I really need to iron the sheets?" And, the answer came back a resounding, "No!"

That's a clear soul message. Honor it. *Bagging* it is about being conscious of what you're doing and why you're doing it. It's a fabulous way to prune unnecessary tasks.

B #2 = Barter It?

Can I barter this task?

In other words, is there someone else who enjoys doing this task more than you? For instance, can you trade jobs with someone or pay them to do the task?

One afternoon, I grumbled about how much I *hated* emptying the dishwasher. My daughter's ears perked up. "What's to hate about emptying the dishwasher, Mom?" Like a leopard who has just discovered his prey at the watering hole, I carefully stalked around the perimeter of the situation.

"Oh yeah? What do *you* hate doing?"

"Folding laundry," she blurted out without missing a beat. "Hate it!" What???? That's like my *all-time* favorite household chore. I knew we were about to strike a bargain that would improve the quality of my life the likes of which I hadn't felt since I bought my robot vacuum (and don't even get started on my love affair with it).

"So," I ventured, "How about from now on, you empty the dishwasher, and I fold laundry?" She snapped up that deal faster than a frog swallows a fly. To this day, as I sit blissfully folding laundry on my bed, watching reruns of "Little House on the Prairie," and listen to the clink of dishes being returned to their rightful homes in our kitchen, I guarantee both of us are thinking the exact same thought, at the same time.

"Sucker."

Or, as the more enlightened would say, "It's a win/win."

The other way you can barter? Pay someone else to do a Dreaded Duty you despise. At one of my seminars, a young surgeon fretted about spending several hours every Sunday afternoon transcribing dictated patient notes. She wished she could use the "3 Bs" to dissolve that massive task and earn a day of rest. A colleague piped in and suggested hiring transcribers in India for an incredibly reasonable price to do the work.

Someone else would be happy to get paid to do what she dreaded.

B #3 = Better It?

What can I do to make this better?

In other words, how can I look for ways to make this experience more pleasant?

My friend Riley, a high school teacher, had grown extremely weary of grading writing assignments for her freshman English class. Her mounting resentment over the monotony of trudging through the typo-laden content from her pubescent authors began to impact her teaching. I had to agree scrawling "INANE" in red ink all over an essay isn't probably the best way to inspire a young writer to further his or her craft.

So, we brainstormed some ways to better this DD for Riley. How could she make grading essays more pleasant, more enjoyable, and more positive? Here's what she came up with:

- If at all possible, find a spot to do the grading outside. Being outdoors always makes Riley feel more grounded, calmer, and brighter.
- Play some terrific classical music in the background. That feels soothing and helps her focus.
- Sip a cup of her favorite chai while she grades.

- Make plans to take a long walk with a friend around the lake near her house when she's done.
- Connect to something she likes about each student before she starts reading his or her paper. That feels good.

My interpretation of the 3 Bs really boils down to one thing: When you focus on the possibility of moving *through* a DD, instead of obsessing over how much you don't want to do it, it feels better. When you feel better, you're going to get more stuff done.

Remember, lots of us have an *old* story playing on an old record player in our heads. We believe that in order to accomplish a challenging task it has to feel *hard*. If it feels even a little pleasant, somehow it doesn't count. *Bettering* is all about giving ourselves permission to enjoy even when we're doing something we're supposed to hate. It's about believing we deserve to switch gears and make the ride less grueling.

Now, go back to your list of DDs from earlier in the chapter. See if you can apply the 3 Bs.

Task #1 _____

Bag it? _____

Barter it?_____

Better it?_____

Task #2 _____

Bag it? _____

Barter it?_____

Better it?_____

Task #3 _____

Bag it? _____

Barter it?_____

Better it?_____

Task #4 _____

Bag it? _____

Barter it?_____

Better it?_____

Task #5 _____

Bag it? _____

Barter it?_____

Better it?_____

C.E.O., visionary, and intuitive genius Bridgette Boudreau says using this tool can help create a big shift in our lives. She says, "The three Bs also start to engage your mind creatively. We stop just moving through our day and reacting to whatever is coming up, and we start to be more intentional about 'What do I want to create in this day?'"

Front-to-Back Method

If you have a DD that's been cumulatively piling up for a while, tackling it can begin to feel futile. We begin to believe we're so far behind we'll never catch up. My client Andy had piles of unprocessed reports, dating back several months, stacked high all over his desk. Every time he sat down to tackle one, an emotional cocktail of annoyance, antsyness, and malaise bubbled up.

Andy felt trapped in an avalanche of paperwork. He had always thrived in his career. Now he no longer looked forward to coming to work. Every time he started in on the most recent reports, he thought about how far behind he'd fallen and how long it would take him to whittle his way down to the oldest reports. Every time he started at the bottom of his pile and began processing his oldest reports, he thought about the new ones accumulating on the top of the pile.

So, we devised a plan to dissipate his DDs, allowing

him to move *through* them, and onto things that held more meaning, purpose, and fun. I call it the Front-to-Back Method. It's as simple as it sounds.

Andy created a turtle step of processing five reports at a time. It felt ridiculously easy. He *bettered* the experience by playing really intense club music while he worked.

He processed his three newest reports first. Then, he tackled the two oldest reports on his desk. Once he got rolling, momentum took over. He had 20 reports processed in a couple of hours. For the first time in a long time, he looked forward to coming to work the next day. In a little over a week, he had his entire desk cleared.

Other clients have used this method for doing everything from assembling photo albums spanning twenty years to organizing decades' worth of financial records. It can be really effective for anything with a chronology that's gotten backlogged.

Work vs. Play

Another method of dealing with DDs is really about semantics. It boils down to the question "Do I want to *work* at something, or *play* with it?" For me, nothing highlights the contrast between work and play more than vacation season, when many of us are either: *a)* counting the minutes until we can stop working and enjoy some rest and relaxation, or *b)* lamenting the fact we're back at work (or back to the work of maintaining life at home) and our play time is over.

We have a primal need to play. Spend a little time watching any nature channel and you'll see lion cubs chase and tumble, monkeys teasing each other, and those insatiable river otters frolicking their days away. Play is part of the natural process of life. But, for most of us, work and play are *very* different. When we're playing, we're dreading work. When we're working, we're dreaming of playing. The main difference between work and play? Our state of mind. I am more relaxed, open, focused, and pleasant when I'm playing. Many of my clients describe feeling tense, serious, distracted, frustrated, and constricted when they're working—the opposite of how they feel when they're playing.

Some time ago, when my coach told me to replace the word *work* with *play* in my life, I nearly blew a gasket. To the cynical journalist in me, this seemed:

a. silly

b. futile

c. very cheesy

Still, somehow, she convinced me to begrudgingly give it a try (probably mostly just to prove her wrong). My coach asked me what I planned to do over the next few days. I told her I needed to seriously work on my website. I had fallen way behind (According to whom? I don't know. But, that's a whole 'nother story) and I needed to spend four hours (minimum!) on my site.

I had officially retired from my commercial freelance gigs and spokesperson work. My website would be the vehicle to unleash my new career on the world. I needed to get going on it.

Only, working on it felt, well, like work.

It felt heavy, and steeped in "have tos" and launched from a place of lack and inadequacy. My inner critic kept barking things like:

"Now that you've ended your other contracts, you have no money coming in!"

"You'll never get enough clients to make a go of this coaching thing unless you do this website right."

"Who are YOU to do this?"

Anyway, in spite of these gloom and doom fears, I agreed to give up working on my site, to play a little. Lo and behold, *playing* on my website felt a lot freer and more creative than working on it. In the few hours that flew by, I had more accomplished than I'd managed to achieve in weeks of slogging away at my work.

Playing with my paperwork and bookkeeping felt way more fun than working on them, too. Same thing with yard-play and houseplay. (Although I haven't yet convinced my daughters it's really homeplay they're doing after school.)

Defining what we're doing as play instead of work brings a lightness and a brighter spirit, which is often where our best, most creative, productive, and efficient results emerge. It also makes it more likely we are in our three Cs zone; calm, clear, and connected.

When I committed to writing this book, I decided to calendar my writing time to turtle step my way through the creative process. The first few days of scheduled writing appointments slipped away and nary a word had made its way onto my manuscript. I took a second to ponder why I didn't seem to "have time" to write.

When I looked at my calendar, there it was, in black and white: "work on book." My subconscious said "Yuck!" and conveniently found ways to distract me from my goal. Instead, it now says "play on book" on my calendar. It feels much better. I still find ways to occasionally procrastinate or distract myself out of sitting down at my computer. But it sure feels better when I see it on my calendar.

"Wait a minute," you may be saying, "Sometimes stuff is just hard. It doesn't feel like a whoosh down the slide at the park, or a game of Pachisi." True. But, remember, there are all kinds of play. Any master musician can attest that being a virtuoso doesn't just happen. It comes from *playing* a lot of music. It doesn't have to be work *or* play. Take an open spirit, a sense of enjoyment, and the desire for pleasant fulfillment into your work today. Go ahead, whistle while you play. You won't have to play at it long before you start feeling a whole lot better, and your DDs seem a whole lot easier.

Take Your Time

When we're trying to move through DDs, the last thing we want to do is languish in them. Savoring doing my taxes? Are you nuts? Most of us are all about racing through the stuff we aren't so wacky about doing. A brisk pace is fine, as long as it doesn't speed up to a frenzy. When we're frenzied, it means we are subconsciously creating imaginary deadlines in our brains.

What's the problem with that? Well, when we are in a hurry, it often means we are in full "fight or flight" mode. When we tell ourselves "hurry up" stories, we often base them in *lack*. DDs can be big triggers for our *not enough time* stories. When we let ourselves get sucked back into the time-sucking vortex created by *not enough time* stories, we may be subconsciously multiplying the number of DDs we need to do.

Fundraising consultant Beth Herman articulates it beautifully: "I am amazed at how well I get things done when I am not spinning anxious stories about other people, the past, the future, and how 'behind' I am." She goes on to say, "I am also noticing that if I dedicate 1/2 hour or 1 hour to a task and excuse myself from any and all distractions, it is always more than enough time. It's the hurrying thoughts that slow me down."

It reminds me of the old saying I heard from my rather grumpy but wise and seasoned 5th grade teacher: "The hurrieder I get, the more behind I get."

Habits

One of my favorite ways to get rid of DDs is to create a habit so you don't even really think about doing it. Charles Duhigg, author of the bestselling "The Power of Habit," cites numerous research studies that show us we use significantly less mental effort when we perform an action out of habit.

Habits are things we do without really thinking about them. They happen without a ton of effort. They come from a place of ease. We don't have to gear up to do something that's become a habit; it just kind of flows. For our purposes, we're going to focus on creating good habits that pave the way for more ease and help us redistribute time toward meaningful, "soul food" activities. Breaking bad habits is a whole separate book (or series of books, depending on how fun you are).

Janine Adams, professional organizer and habit expert says, "When you create habits and incorporate them into routines, you'll be amazed at how much you can accomplish on a regular basis."

Tips for creating new habits:

1. Piggybacking

The easiest way to start a new habit is to hook it to a habit you already have. My client Maggie had a whole list of self-improvement goals for herself. And she had a catalog of stories about how all of her previous attempts to make these changes had failed. So, I asked her to give me a short list of the habits she already had, the stuff she did every day, no matter what.

Maggie's Habits

- Brushing her teeth (morning and night)
- Putting in her contacts (morning)
- Taking out her contacts (evening)
- Emptying the dishwasher (morning)
- Loading the dishwasher (after dinner)

Your habits.

List things you do every day.

Start in the morning and imagine your routines throughout the day.

_____

_____

_____

_____

_____

_____

_____

_____

Next, I asked Maggie to list the new habits she'd like to form.

Maggie's New Habits

- Drinking her wheatgrass shots (her grandma's cure for a long life)
- Flossing her teeth
- Sorting the mail daily and clearing it off the catch-all counter in her kitchen
- Using sunscreen

New Habits You'd Like to Form

_____

_____

_____

_____

_____

_____

_____

Once she'd written them down, Maggie had an easy time piggybacking the habits she'd like to form with her old ones.

- Right after she brushes her teeth in the morning, she flosses
- Right after she puts her contacts in, she puts sunscreen on her face
- After she unloads the dishwasher in the morning, she drinks her wheatgrass (don't judge)
- After she loads the dishwasher in the evening, she sets her timer for 5 minutes (turtle steps, baby) and quickly sorts the day's mail and clears off the counter

Now, go back up to your "Old Habits" list and take your new habits and piggyback them.

Old Habit piggybacked with New Habit

_____

_____

_____

_____

_____

_____

_____

Six months later, Maggie reports all of her piggybacked new habits have become old hat. What worked this time that didn't work the other times she tried to form them? She didn't make them stand alone as tasks she needed to think about and rev up to start. Instead, now, they just happen without her thinking about them.

2. Connect to the reward

There's a whole lot of research on habits (the good variety, and the not-so-good variety) that shows we are more likely to create a habit when we receive a reward for doing it. Someone doesn't have to present you with an Oscar for putting your laundry away. However, if you take a minute to consciously connect to what you like and appreciate about completing the task that you're trying to form into a habit, it can help.

For instance, Maggie made a conscious effort to examine her gums when she got done flossing. Seems silly. But, after a few days, her gums stopped bleeding. She knew that meant they were healthier and she was reaping the benefits of her new habit. She also took a minute to appreciate the cleared space on her previously cluttered counter. Just noticing that helped her feel like there was a little more calm and a little less chaos in her life.

3. Don't Break the Chain

Habits are developed through repetition. You've probably heard it takes 21 days to form a habit. There isn't much research to back up this claim. As a matter of fact, one European study on habits found it took participants between 18 and 254 days to form a new one.

Still, I find if I do something for three to four weeks, it begins to feel more like a routine and a habit. Jerry Seinfeld is said to have coined one of the most famous habit forming techniques out there. It's called "Don't Break the Chain." The story says someone once asked the comedian how he managed to churn out so much good writing. He said he decided to make a habit out of writing. Every day he wrote, he marked his calendar with a big red X. Over time, he didn't want to break the chain of red X's on his calendar. So, he kept going, and the habit was formed.

You can do this with a good old-fashioned paper calendar and a red marker. Or, if you prefer digital options, I like **www.HabitForge.com** and the "Don't Break the Chain" app for your smartphone.

Chapter 8

Creating Time for What You Love

I may sound like a broken record, but my agenda for you is *not* to be the best darn list crosser-offer or task completer in the universe. It is to help free you from suffering at the hands of the clock, so you can create more time to do the stuff you love; the stuff that makes your heart sing and makes the world a better place.

When you create time to do what you love, you create more flow in your life, and you increase your satisfaction, improve your relationships, and make it more likely you'll experience productivity and accomplishment.

Starving yourself from doing what you love is *not* the solution to getting more done. Being resentful, discouraged, and feeling inadequate keep you from doing all you can do to be all you can be in this one life you have to live.

Busting Busy

To unravel the chaos that is blocking you from doing what you enjoy, you need to examine what's making things so hectic. Some of you have read this entire book, thinking, "A lot of this stuff sounds dandy, but I'm just too darn *busy* to give anything new a try."

After a discussion my friend Kara and I had about the concept of busyness, she conducted a little experiment. She asked the first ten people she bumped in to how they were doing and/or what they'd been up to lately. All ten of them answered "busy" or (one of its derivatives, "unbelievably busy," "so busy,""busy, as always," and "crazy busy") to both questions.

In other words, 100% of the respondents in this impromptu survey used *busy* as the primary descriptor to characterize the state of their well-being, and to sum up their activities. And Kara wasn't in an urban E.R. or at a bead stand during Mardi Gras where we would expect the respondents to be super busy.

Nope. She was right in the middle of suburbia, talking to regular moms like me.

Don't get me wrong. I understand that certain phases and timeframes in life are inherently busy. Moving day, tax deadlines, the week before a wedding, or hurricane evacuation are not periods in our lives when most of us are basking in oodles of quiet reflective time.

The disconnect has happened because many of us are as busy on any given Saturday as an air traffic controller during a raging thunderstorm So, who are these busy people? "It's almost always people whose lamented busyness is purely self-imposed: work and obligations they've taken on voluntarily, classes and activities they've 'encouraged' their kids to participate in. They're busy because of their own ambition or drive or anxiety, because they're addicted to busyness and dread what they might have to face in its absence," writes author and cartoonist Tim Kreider in an opinion piece for the New York Times.

Busy as an Identity

Poet M.E. Tuthill says we worship at the altar of busy. In the words of the legendary Henry David Thoreau, "It is not enough if you are busy. The question is, 'What are you busy about?'"

When it boils right down to it, lots of us have slipped into a pattern in which we're afraid of *not* being busy. Busy has become our worth-o-meter. We have begun to believe that busier makes us better—or, we subscribe to the opposite belief, that un-busyness makes us inadequate.

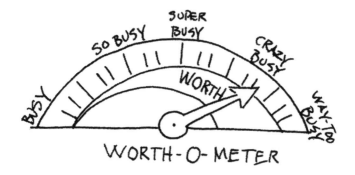

WORTH-O-METER

I love what blogger Anastasiya Goers says: "Many people enter a race of 'Who can be the busiest today?' Our kids are busy with all possible after-school activities. We take on social commitments and new tasks just to cram more accomplishments in our day. Unfortunately, no matter how much we accomplish and how busy we remain, we do not experience happiness or joy. It drains us and we lose connection to the things that really matter."

Our fear brain feeds us thoughts like:

"The busier I am, the better I am."

"If I'm not busy, I'm not doing enough."

"I need to be busy, or people will think I'm lazy."

"Being busy makes me count."

Despite the convincing tone of our inner critic, these connections between our busyness and our worth are a big fat pack of lies. Some of the busiest people I know are contributing very little to the good of themselves, their families, their communities, or the world. They've become so obsessed with being busy, they've lost touch with any sense of meaning behind their existence. They've forgotten their "why."

The Stats

Many parents report feeling too busy to properly connect to their kids. A 2011 survey showed 88% of working parents suffer stress-related health problems. However, another study, published by researchers in California, reported that the amount of time parents are spending caring for their children has *increased* dramatically since the 1990s. In 1995, moms spent about 12 hours a week exclusively tending to the needs of their children. By 2007, that number had risen to more than 21 hours per week. So, it appears we're actually spending more time with our kids—but we're so attached to our "busy beyond belief" stories, we aren't aware that we're doing it.

It can happen to any of us. Our egos want us to believe these busy lies. We look for ways to boast of our busyness. We compare ourselves to others and try to impress with tales of whose life if more insane.

Amy Ahlers, best-selling author of "Big Fat Lies Women Tell Themselves," says, "We wear overwhelm like a badge of honor."

Deanna Kienast, my favorite abstract artist and a wild-ly successful entrepreneur says, "People have programmed themselves to think because their cell phone is constantly vi-brating, they are so busy."

Nick Ortner, an expert in helping people heal from emo-tional pain says, at some point, each person needs to realize, "I don't need overwhelm to feel valuable." He says many of us believe we need to feel overwhelmed, burned out, and fren-zied to deserve what we earn. We begin to believe nothing counts unless it's the product of crazed frenzy.

Most of us spend our lives hiding behind a veil of too busy. It's a safe place to keep from stepping out on the stage.

As Brooke Castillo says, "'Busy' is the generalized excuse we use for not going after our dreams."

Busy as an Excuse

I hear it all the time, "Jill, I'd LOVE to spend more time praying, meditating, reading, spending time with friends, exercising, (fill in the blank, here)…but, I'm just too *busy*."

Here's the big news. Being busy is a choice.

Ouch, there you go screaming, "You're so flipping *wrong*, Jill," in your head at me again. That's okay, I can hack it. Take a deep breath and play along for just a minute.

Remember, way back in Chapter 3, in tip #6 for your to-do list makeover, when I first introduced you to the idea of "have to" verses "choose to"? Do you recall how the only thing we really *have* to do every day is breathe? Everything else is a choice.

Again, I totally understand that most of us forget, or at least our fear-brains conveniently forget, but our level of busyness is *also* a choice. Tim Kreider also writes, "Busyness serves as a kind of existential reassurance, a hedge against emptiness; obviously your life cannot possibly be silly or trivial or meaningless if you are so busy, completely booked, in demand every hour of the day."

Unwinding the Busy

Trey, a client with a fast-paced career in the entertainment industry, bristled when I challenged his "I'm too busy to do anything for *myself*," story. I asked Trey to rate his busyness on a scale of 1 to 10. "Eleven," he said.

He indignantly reminded me that if he didn't take care of his clients, his business would fold. I asked Trey to list what had him so busy. Here's what he wrote:

1. Client phone calls
2. Client e-mails
3. Project development

4. House stuff

5. Kid/family stuff

6. Making sure everyone is happy.

You don't have to be a life coach to see #6 on his list is where Trey may have been tripping himself up. His fear of others' disapproval (his family, his clients, even his competitors) rendered him unable to risk being still. So, I asked Trey to try an experiment. For just a week, I encouraged him to focus on the things that made *him* happy. His list:

1. Creating fabulous scripts

2. Project development planning

3. Being outside in the sunshine

4. Laughing with his kids

5. Clearing off his desk

6. Working out

Reluctantly, he agreed to give it a shot. But, he was quite sure if he focused on the list of things that made him happy, he would fall woefully behind at work, and his business would crumble.

However, a week later, Trey was amazed at how energized he felt. On a scale of 1 to 10, I asked him to rate how busy he'd been the previous week. "About a 4," he said. Yet, even though he reported being so much less busy, Trey's productivity was off the charts. He finished an entire script in a week. Ideas flowed so fast, he couldn't write them all down. He had meetings scheduled and investors already jazzed about some of his recently birthed concepts. He had more fun with his wife and kids than he remembered in a long time. He'd even stayed fairly on top of his e-mail.

Why the enormous shift? Trey didn't stop doing everything. He just started doing things that made his soul sing. Everything felt in better alignment and flowed better in that space. Remember the 3 Cs: calm, clear, connected? Trey's experience was terrific proof that's the best place to get stuff done.

When he became brave enough to step away from his default mode, "crazy busy," and create time to be intentional, things got better. Busy was a choice that had not been serving him.

Scary Stories

As we talked about in Chapter 4, fight or flight mode causes us to be less efficient, challenges our ability to be clear and civil in our communication and relationships with others, and generally heightens fear and anger reactions (not to mention what it's doing to our bodies. Oy, the stress hormones. Poison, I tell ya.)

See the cycle, here? If we stop the incessant spinning for just a second, we can see scary stories are often the launching places of our busyness.

Fear = What if other kids end up better, smarter, faster than my kids?

Result = Overprogrammed children who suffer from anxiety-induced mental and physical illness at shockingly early ages.

Fear = If my friends are busier than me, other people will think they are more successful.

Result = Ramping up activity to the point of constant motion. Adrenal burnout, enormous amounts of stress hormones coursing through your veins, physical breakdown, and disease (not to mention lack of contentment.)

Fear = If I'm not busy, then things will fall apart.

Result = Severe control issues and the inability to relax and assume things will work out.

What are you afraid will happen if you stop being busy? _____

_____

What's the results of your constant busyness? __

_____

Is it serving you? _____

Is it serving anyone else? _____

List Three Things you can do that make you happy that are currently being squeezed out by your busyness:

1. _____

2. _____

3. _____

Now, conduct an experiment. For a week, do each of the things that you listed above. Notice what happens to your contentment *and* to your productivity.

To wrap this up with our previous discussions on procrastination, the simplest way for me to say this is that excuses for being too busy to do what we *really* want to do are really just fear dressed up as something else. "Too busy" excuses are our way of avoiding what we're afraid we can't do perfectly. Often, we're afraid of putting ourselves out there.

We're afraid we might not get everyone's approval if we do something. So, we hide behind "too busy."

Summertime... Where the Livin' Is Crazy

Barb came to me *really* frustrated, frazzled, and fried. Where were the lazy, hazy days of summer? Instead of relaxing by the pool, she was running on a sizzling hot treadmill without a stop button; coaxing kids out of bed, packing for camps, ferrying to and from a seemingly endless array of sports or other "enrichment" activities, and trying to hammer out vacation details. And that was all before 8:15 on a Tuesday morning, *before* she went to work.

Barb and her husband felt like pinballs in a machine— bounced and paddled around with the threat of being sucked down a chute if they stopped moving. After listening to Barb's dilemma and realizing it felt *really* familiar to me, I came up with three steps to help put the fun back into summer. It's a tool that I use all year 'round these days.

You'll notice that these tips incorporate much of what we've talked about in previous chapters. They're distilled into what I call my **F.I.T.** plan. It only takes about 5 minutes in the morning.

1. **Feeling state** – Take a minute to decide what feeling state you'd like to create for the day. Do you want to be peaceful, quiet, and contemplative, or peppy and productive? Or do you want to feel connected, joyful, and efficient? Once you decide, *consciously* create ways to make that happen. Better feeling states lead to better days.

2. **Intentionality** – Look at your calendar and then your to-do list. Be calm, *intentional*, and curious. Does *everything* really need to be done today? Or have you just used "stream of consciousness" list-making to vomit up an array of tasks and events that leave you feeling defeated at the end of the day? Being *intentional* means looking at your *actual time available* (not the time you "wish" you had or "should" have) and calmly and consciously planning your day to MAINTAIN THE FEELING STATE you chose in step #1, above. Use the structure from our to-do list makeover in Chapters 2 & 3 to help maintain your positive intentions.

3. **Time for yourself** – Every single day, put some time for yourself on your calendar. It can be 10 minutes or 10 hours. Pick an amount of time, and a time of day that feel good to you. But make sure you treat that time as sacred and honor

this commitment to yourself no matter what is going on. I try to put something on the calendar that I can **only** do this time of year (see Chapter 3 for more on this.)

F.I.T. worked great for Barb. After she started using it, when someone asked her how her summer was going, she caught herself before blurting out, "Crazy!" or "Nuts!" like she'd done for the entire month of June. Instead, she paused and said, "It's going really well. I've committed to enjoy the stuff that makes this time of year so unique."

Pushing Pause

This all boils down to two questions: What's it all for? Why are you doing it all?

When we let ourselves get sucked into the busy machine, we often find our constant motion spins us into butter, when we really wanted to be cream. I love this oft-used quote from billionaire Malcolm Forbes, "By the time we've made it, we've had it." It reminds us that doing for the sake of doing burns us out. It can separate us from our true selves in the name of achievement.

However, the goal is not inertia. Being active and achieving are not our enemies. Quite the contrary. Inspired action that connects to a purpose that is in alignment with our soul (or essential self, or the unique person that God created us to be) is magical. It can mean working really hard, being fully engaged for long stretches of time, and using our minds and bodies until we are bone tired.

Being busy for the sake of busy is not magical. It's soul sucking.

Martha Beck says, "The problem is that perpetually doing, without ever tuning in to the center of our being, is the equivalent of fueling a mighty ship by tossing all its navigational equipment into the furnace."

Keys to Inspired Action

Ways to keep yourself from getting sucked into a busy addiction.

1. Ask yourself: Does this nourish me, or deplete me?

2. Believe that you are equally worthy whether you are busy or still.

3. Recognize that you deserve time for rest, time to reboot, and time to do what you love.

I love what creativity expert Jill Winski says: "What we really mean when we say 'there's not enough time' is: I'm trying to outrun my painful thoughts about not accomplishing enough. I've got to hurry up. So, let me add more and more to my to-do list. If we let ourselves be done, we're admitting we're enough. Our painful thoughts don't like that acceptance."

She goes on to say, "I'm going to suggest that the 'time issue' is not about time, at all. It's really about our stressful thought that, at some point, our lives will be over and won't have done what we wanted to do with them. It's really about our lack of self-acceptance, about the fact that we're afraid to meet ourselves, to accept ourselves, exactly where we are. It's about a belief that there's a finish line we should have crossed years ago, and we haven't even made our way out of the starting gate."

A New Relationship

Bottom line, it's time to divorce yourself from your dysfunctional relationship with busy. Instead, begin to foster a new connection to the things you love. Don't remember what you love to do because it's been so long since you let yourself enjoy something? Then give yourself the gift of dabbling. Date around, so to speak, until you find something that lights you up. Discover a hobby. You may end up discovering a passion. Or, you could just have fun for a while and then move on to something else.

Be "on to yourself" when you are busying your life away. Be conscious of the reasons behind your busyness. Notice if you are using your busyness as a worth-o-meter. Be intentional and create time for things that nourish your soul.

Next, try the ultimate test: Dare to be the *least* busy person you know. Your competitors in the "who can be the busiest" contest may not approve of your blatant calm, clarity, and contentment—but I have a hunch you'll still feel like a winner.

Chapter 9

At the End Of the Day

Not long ago, as I got ready for bed one night at our cabin, I started thinking about all of the stuff I *hadn't* gotten done. I suddenly felt deflated and antsy. My end-of-day assessment had completely drained the joy out of my day.

There's no question, as we discussed in previous chapters, that "achievement" is one of the parts of our lives that contributes to our well-being. (For much more on this read up on Martin Seligman's work at the University of Pennsylvania.) However, a lot of perfectly good days are ruined after twilight by our judgmental evaluation of what's transpired (or hasn't transpired). This post-game analysis can suck the fun out of any day. If we're not careful, our whole life can pass us by that way.

At the End of Our Days

Not long ago, my friend Brett shared that he feared his dad had lost his will to live. "The thing that's really frustrating is that the doctors say he's in amazing health for 85. His heart is strong, his mind is sharp, his hearing is good," Brett explained. "He hasn't faced the physical challenges of most of his peers. But his newly diagnosed vertigo means he has to slow down. No big garden to tend in the heat and no more climbing up on ladders. My Dad says if he's not *doing* enough, there's no reason to live."

Our culture wants us to believe that if we're not doing, we might as well cease being. I believe that was the source of Walter's malaise and discouragement.

As I've said before, achieving and accomplishing can be beautiful, wonderful things that increase our endorphins and help us to impact the world around us for good. The goal is *not* to stop doing everything and sit in meditation (or in front of your plasma screen TV or computer) all day for years on end.

But, it can be powerful to recognize that doing, achieving, and accomplishing can take on many forms.

Take the example of my day at the lake where I didn't think I'd gotten enough done. Here's how my mind framed things at the end of that day:

What I didn't get accomplished:

- Sweeping
- Editing
- Laundry
- Veggie chopping
- Reading for work
- Walking my five mile loop

What I *did* get done.

- Water skiing (on amazing water—which, by the way, is good exercise)
- Lots of laughter with my girls
- Losing myself in a fascinating novel
- Experiencing a fantastic sunset

Now, at the end of my life, will I look at these two lists and wish I had done more on the top one?

More laundry and fewer sunsets?

I don't think so. Yet, my old stories about doing enough robbed me of savoring the soul-enriching experiences I did have.

The Key Questions

As we wrap up our brief, yet abundant time together, I'd love for you to consider some key questions to help you get more time, satisfaction, joy, love, and impact out of this one precious life you have to live.

Why?

We begin with the most important one.

Why are you doing what you're doing?

We have touched on this in several places in this book. Because, if you can answer this question, you can usually identify the culprit that's costing you time, keeping you stuck, and stalling your motivation. Knowing your "why" is key.

If you are trying to motivate yourself to do things from a place of beating yourself up, you will likely spin your wheels. Or, you will burn yourself out to the point of mental exhaustion. Eventually your body will say *no* in the form of physical disease and decline.

To achieve the unique things you were put on this earth to do, in the ways you were created to serve yourself and others, you must launch your action from a purpose that's connected to your highest, most loving self. Doing for the sake of doing or anything that's purely entrenched in the material or ego-driven world will ultimately feel empty, unsatisfying, and worthless.

Why is it worth the effort to figure out why you're doing something?

Ultimately, I believe we all crave meaning, worth and purpose in our lives. We sometimes try to satisfy that craving with purely ego-driven action. That's like trying to get full on cotton candy. It might taste good for a minute, but in the end, it will never truly satisfy, and it could make you sick in the process. Ego-driven action that's shrouded in a heavy fear of inadequacy causes us to hide out in procrastination or perfectionism-driven paralysis, starving our souls from experiencing meaning or growth. As Dyana Valentine, speaker and inspirer extraordinaire says, "We are so much more than what we do. Our why is our treasure."

The balance comes in rooting and connecting ourselves to a higher purpose that lines up with our unique gifts and abilities. And then actually taking the leap, even when it feels a little scary, to make something happen. Which leads us to our next question.

What?

What is it you are doing? What actions are you taking? What are you choosing to do to fill your time?

When you have a clear understanding of why you are doing something, and that "why" is clearly connected to your highest purpose, the discernment process of what to do gets easier in many ways. You are able to more clearly see what actions are the most efficient, effective, and purposeful way to make the most of your time.

When you are selective about *what* you are doing, you begin to say no to things that don't serve your highest purpose. That can be frightening. If you dare to say "no" more than once, people may stop asking you to be in charge of the committee to form the committee that created the committee at your kids' school, for instance. Your ego may whimper about not feeling needed.

It will get over it.

Trust me. Those around you may fuss if you dare to create some boundaries and stop martyring yourself by doing things that don't serve your highest purpose. They'll eventually get over it, too.

"Live by faith, not by sight. Living your purpose will require a HUGE amount of faith, courage, tenacity, and perseverance," says Mastin Kipp, founder of The Daily Love.

The best way to make sure what you're doing is productive and meaningful is to revisit our prioritization zones (see Chapter 2 or the quick reference at the end of the book.) Getting in the right zone is the best way to take yourself off the hamster wheel of frenetic circular motion or out of that stuck, unfulfilled place, and into the zone you want to be in.

Ultimately, when you stop believing the *not enough time* lie (revisit Chapter 4, if need be), then you are able to access that calm, clear, and connected state where discernment gets so much easier. It just gets a lot less complicated to decide what to do. You will get more done in less time when you focus your efforts on *what* really matters.

We'll tackle *how* to do that next.

How?

Let's go back to our bottom line.

How do you get more time in your life? How can you find time to do the things you love? I've distilled it down into a cheat sheet of sorts for you.

1. Notice when you are having *there's not enough time* and all related thoughts ("I need more time," "There isn't enough time," "I'm too busy," etc.). Be conscious and mindful of that thought, without beating yourself up. Simply say, "I *notice* I'm having the 'There's not enough time' thought again.'" Also, notice in what other areas in your life you may be feeling lack. When we're worried about money, other people's approval, or any of the other things our

fear mind loves to conjure up scary stories about, time is almost always sure to run in short supply, too. Notice these scary stories. Identify them, and say "I notice I'm having the "There's not enough_____ thought, again." It's like shining a light on something that's been casting a huge shadow over you and discovering it's not a monstrous dragon that's threatening you, but a measly little gecko.

2. Replace the unhelpful, sabotaging *there's not enough time* with *there IS enough time* and notice how your ability to problem-solve skyrockets. Notice how much more efficient you are when you are tapped into abundance, versus mired in scarcity. Notice how your brain begins to scan for and harvest opportunity, instead of being magnetized to problems and roadblocks. There *IS* enough time!

3. Create turtle steps to get momentum rolling. Just start. Notice when you're telling yourself you need a bigger chunk of time to do something. Those stories keep us immobile. Breaking a project down into ridiculously easy steps is the best way to tackle it. No step is too small; the simpler, the better.

4. Use a to-do list to help you stay in your lane. Limit it to five things. Put specific tasks for specific times of day on your calendar when you can. Base your to-do list on your available time.

5. Don't be afraid to barter things out. You don't have to do it all. You can also be intentional about looking for ways to make tasks you don't love more enjoyable. It doesn't make a job less important or make it count less if you are somewhat content while you do it.

Wrap Up

Back to Walter, the octogenarian who was ready to call it quits. Brett began helping his dad look for ways to use the wealth of his wisdom to reach out to others. He connected some of his friends, enthusiastic but novice gardeners, to his dad. They were amazed at his vast, homespun knowledge. (He was amazed at how much money Brett's friends spent on a hobby they knew so little about. But, that's a whole 'nother story.)

Anyway, instead of hyperfocusing on what he was not getting done, talking to Brett's friends about gardening helped Walter connect to a purpose that had meaning and impact to him. He wasn't doing what he'd always done. But, he was doing good, for sure. You can't always write the script for your life. But you can choose how you react to the plot twists.

Some people tell me they are afraid if they make these shifts, they won't get as much done. But, many of my clients have bravely unraveled their own lies about time, and the results are humbling and amazing to witness.

Some of my favorites:

- A corporate bigwig who used to be up every night worrying constantly about how much more time she needed to get everything done. Now that she's begun to believe time is abundant, she's more relaxed and calmer than she's ever been. Her productivity is off the charts.
- A physician, considered a leader in his field, who is making time for real vacations for the first time in more than twenty years.
- A stay-at-home mom friend who started selling her art, just because it lights her up, *and* so she can afford to hire a cleaning lady (because cleaning does not light her up).
- A woman who went from being the hand-wringing spouse of a husband whose business was in ruins to a successful business owner in her own right. She's stopped feeling overwhelmed and not capable. She has turtle-stepped her way into a thriving direct sales company.

- A doctor client who has used the 3 Bs to declutter her entire house and office.
- A therapist who used the to-do list makeover to stop spinning his wheels and create meaningful progress in a health and wellness program he'd been ruminating about for years.

My intention for you is to take the ideas and tools in this little book and change the world.

How do you do that?

When you tap into that calm, clear, connected space—that place where you experience your most amazing work and play—there is no limit to the magic you can create. Take the power away from the time lies that have ruled your life and logjammed your flow for a long time. Reconnect yourself to love: for yourself, for amazing ideas, for the wonders of the world around you, for beauty, and for the other people who populate the human race.

Trust me, my wonderful friend. There IS enough time.

"Tell me, what is it you plan to do
with your one wild and precious life?"
— Mary Oliver, *New and Selected Poems*

Postscript:

As you take the concepts of this book to heart, you'll begin to see, with crystal-clear clarity, those around you who are suffering un-necessarily from their own time lies. I hope you'll consider sharing this book with them.

My mission: Help make the world a more meaningful place, where time is no longer in short supply. Go forth and create with abundance, my dear friends.

Lots of love,

Jill

For Quick Reference

Prioritization Zones

The Stress-Out Zone

- Urgent matters
- Unexpected crises
- Medical emergencies
- Pressing problems
- Deadline-driven stuff
- Last-minute preparations for scheduled activities

Lots of the items in this zone are necessary. However, they can take over your life if you're not aware and conscious. Spend too much time in this zone, and you will be BURNED OUT.

Manage by being mindful.
Delegate. Barter. Plan. Organize.

The Hamster-on-the-Wheel Zone

- Interruptions
- Some phone calls
- Constant e-mail checking
- Some meetings
- Many "pressing" matters

This is where we get deceived. We get sucked into "doing"— and this zone can trap us if we're not careful. We're constantly moving, and not going anywhere. This is why 2-minute tasks are so important. We keep the little stuff in a container, so it doesn't leak out into other areas and take over.

Avoid when possible. Be specific about and limit the amount of time you spend doing any of the tasks listed above.